OURAY
CHIEF OF THE UTES

*The fascinating story of Colorado's
most famous and controversial
Indian Chief*

by P. David Smith

WESTERN REFLECTIONS PUBLISHING COMPANY®
Lake City, Colorado

Copyright © 1986, 2021

ISBN 978-1-937851-57-6
All rights reserved including the right of reproduction
in any form in whole or in part.

Cover design by Laurie Goralka Design

Cover Painting by Gordon Phillips

Western Reflections Publishing Company
951B North Highway 951
P. O. Box 1149
Lake City, Colo. 81432
(970) 944-0110
www.westernreflectionspublishing.com

To my wife Jan and to my children Tricia, Tami, and Stephen,
I dedicate this book.

Author's Note—Originally, the Ute Indians had no written language. Any spelling of their names was a white man's interpretation of what was being said. As a result, it is not uncommon to see an Indian's name spelled many different ways. I have used the form that seems to be the most common.

Also, I have not corrected spelling or grammar within quotes unless it was necessary to make the sentence understandable.

TABLE OF CONTENTS

Introduction		7
Prologue —	Traitor or Visionary	10
One:	The Utes—The Blue Sky People	14
Two:	The Early Years—New Mexico	34
Three:	The Tabeguache—Ouray's Rise to Power	43
Four:	The Treaty of 1863—Ouray Becomes a Negotiator	59
Five:	The Treaty of 1868—New Agencies	72
Six:	The Brunot Treaty of 1873—Ouray Finds His Son?	91
Seven:	Alferd Packer—The Man-eater	118
Eight:	Los Pinos II—The Uncompahgre Agency	131
Nine:	The Battle of Milk Creek—The Meeker Massacre	154
Ten:	Ouray's Death—The Utes Leave Colorado	179
Eleven:	Chipeta's Last Days—Ouray's Reburial	194
Epilogue		209
Bibliography		211

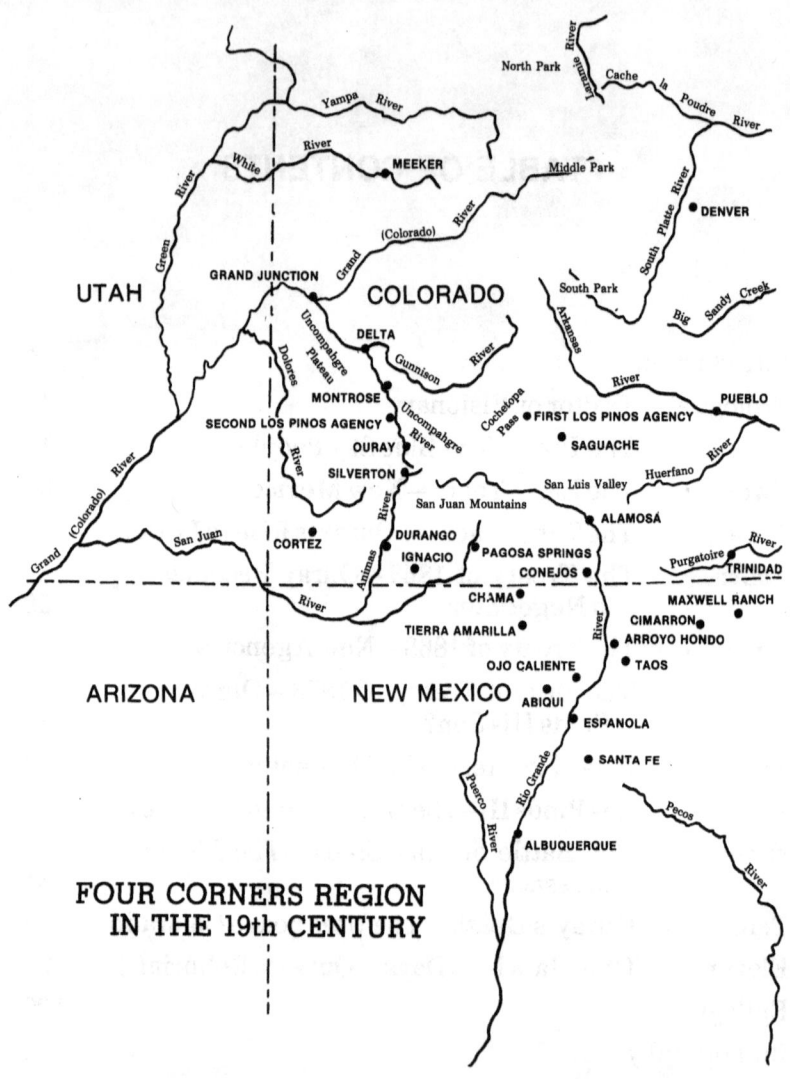

FOUR CORNERS REGION
IN THE 19th CENTURY

By the end of the nineteenth century, most of the towns that now make up the Four Corners area were in existence. The majority of the rivers and mountains had obtained their names centuries before from the Spanish, who had slowly worked their way north from Santa Fe, which was established in 1609. Spaniards were dealing with the Ute Indians for two hundred years before the first trappers and explorers from the United States began to travel in the area. Their first "highways" were rivers because the rushing waters usually carved out gentle slopes that were easy to follow, and because food and water were easy to find along the river.

INTRODUCTION

This biography of Colorado's famous Indian chief (and, I would like to say, one of our most beloved citizens) is the outgrowth of several years of painstaking research and collecting of evidence to either support facts of the chief's life or to set aside some of the myths. There has long been a need for just such a work as this.

In the past, much that has been either written or told about Chief Ouray has been based on assumption or legend—perhaps the most persistent myth being the tale that the burial place of Chief Ouray is a big, dark, mysterious secret. As a matter of fact, almost every year someone comes up with a new, fanciful theory as to the whereabouts of Chief Ouray's remains. The burial place of Ouray is not a secret at all, and the reader of this book will find the true account of the chief's final resting place.

From the time of his arrival in the community, P. David Smith was almost obsessed with a desire to learn more about Ouray, perhaps the greatest of the Indian chiefs. There was little available information about Ouray except that which was scattered in many places, all of which had to be brought together and sorted out. One story would have to be compared with others; writings of men who knew and had dealings with the chief, as well as old newspaper accounts, had to be checked against government records—all in order to amass supporting evidence of what was supposedly known about Chief Ouray. Probably the least dependable sources of information were the old newspapers, for they were extremely biased during Ouray's lifetime, and almost without exception were excessively anti-Indian—"The Utes Must Go!" It is noteworthy, however, that almost never did an editor write disrespectfully of Chief Ouray.

Having been privileged to read Mr. Smith's manuscript before it was submitted to the publisher, and being, myself, a devoted admirer of Chief Ouray, I do not hesitate to pronounce this book the most credible account of the life of this truly great man. I recommend it, not only to the general reader who has a taste for true Western history, but for use in classrooms as well.

Marvin Gregory
Ouray, Colorado

Acknowledgments

To my wife Jan and Doris Swanson for typing and retyping the manuscript;

To Marvin Gregory for many, many hours of discussing Ouray and Chipeta, for reading many of my rough drafts, for allowing me access to unpublished manuscripts in his possession and for writing a good deal of the captions for this book;

To Mary Ann Dismant for her help and encouragement and to her and Jon Jindra for constant help in obtaining the source books needed;

To Roger Henn and Father Richard Doll for reading my rough manuscript for historical accuracy;

To Gordon Phillips for painting the portrait of Ouray and Chipeta used on the front cover and to Clarke Cohu for designing the cover;

To Marvin and Ruth Gregory, The Colorado Historical Society and the Denver Public Library for the photographs used in this book;

And to Jack Swanson and Janet Oslund for editing and generally discussing the concept of the book,

MANY THANKS.

PROLOGUE
TRAITOR OR VISIONARY

High in the rotunda of the State of Colorado Capitol Building are sixteen stained glass portraits which honor outstanding Colorado pioneers. These individuals were chosen because they were Colorado's founding fathers, but one of them is an Indian—Chief Ouray. Not only was an Indian included among the sixteen portraits, but Ouray was also the sole person so honored who received a unanimous vote. It must certainly be unique that an Indian came to be acclaimed for developing a state.

Chief Ouray has generally been treated in history as a hero. However, a true evaluation is difficult because so many contradictory statements have been written about him. Although not a full-blooded Ute, he was appointed by the United States to be the first overall Chief of the Ute Nation. He had no official Ute sanction, but he somehow—perhaps through sheer force of personality—was able to gain the trust and respect of most of his people. Many of his tribe believed in him so completely that they died for him. However, several members of his own tribe (including his own brother-in-law) considered him to be a traitor and tried to kill him. Although he was feared as quick to kill, he is also credited by many as being the greatest Indian peacemaker of all time. Only once during Ouray's rule (during the 1879 Meeker uprising) did the Utes openly rebel against the whites. What was the secret that allowed him to keep the Utes in line? Was it his diplomacy and tact? Was it the threat of instant death if Ouray was crossed? Was it his intellect and wisdom?

The white men of the time, including several presidents of the United States, all felt that Ouray was one of the greatest of the Indian chiefs. Ouray was described by a contemporary as "a man full of magnetism, a man full of gestures" and also by another as "a good man and a man who would have measured up to the highest standards of any community." However, this viewpoint must be tempered, since the prevalent mood of the time was that "the only good Indian was a dead Indian." Most important to the white man was that Ouray was able to keep the dangerous Utes peaceful even in the face of constant lying and mistreatment by the whites. Ouray evidently realized the futility of the Utes fighting the whites and openly advised his people over and over to submit to them. But on the other hand, almost any concession to the United States was bound to include a guarantee of his own personal comfort and authority. Ouray led the Ute nation through its period of greatest turmoil. During his lifetime the Ute dominion was to shrink from the western half of Colorado and eastern Utah to a few small reservations in southwestern Colorado and northeastern Utah. What was even more puzzling was that Ouray was able to sell almost all the Ute territory to the whites at a time when the Indians believed that their land was owned not by the chief but by the tribe as a whole. In fact, the truth was probably closer to a belief that no one owned the land!

To study the life of Ouray is frustrating. There are many inconsistencies. Even such a simple fact as whether or not he could speak English is clouded with controversy. Some writers who met Ouray reported that he spoke fluent English, and yet others who knew him said that they could barely understand him. President Hayes is supposed to have said that Ouray was one of the most intellectual men that he ever conversed with. Most men who knew him acknowledged that Ouray liked to talk and took great pleasure in entering into long, serious conversations.

Unfortunately there is no way to look at Ute records to determine what is factual. The Utes had no written language, and the white man has now spent a century trying to force the Utes to erase the past and forget their heritage. The only documents remaining from which to try to reconstruct Ouray's life are those of the white man. But even the contemporary accounts of Ouray are full of inaccuracies. The same incident was often reported in two very different ways because of the opinions and biases of the reporters. Many writers have unfortunately confused history by writing articles about Ouray which indicate a total lack of knowledge of him or of the Utes. Certainly most of the fluent language attributed by reporters to Ouray could not have come from his mouth. Although intelligent, he had only the equivalent of a second or third grade education. He spoke fluent Spanish but only pidgin English. More than likely, the reporters would take a statement of Ouray's and embellish it in their own way. For example, the following quote is attributed to Ouray:

> I realize the ultimate destiny of my people. They will be extirpated by the race that overruns, occupies and holds our hunting grounds, whose numbers and force, with the government and millions behind it will in a few years remove the last trace of our blood that now remains. We shall fall as the leaves from the trees when frost or winter comes and the lands which we have roamed over for countless generations will be given over to the miner and the plowshare. In place of our humble tepees, the "white man's" towns and cities will appear and we shall be buried out of sight beneath the avalanche of the new civilization. This is the destiny of my people. My part is to protect them

and yours as far as I can, from the violence and bloodshed while I live, and to bring both into friendly relations, so that they may be at peace with one another.

The philosophy is that of Ouray, but the four syllable words and the flowery and poetic phrasing are certainly those of a reporter. The grammar is too good and the sentences are structured too well to be those of one with a second or third grade education who could barely speak English.

All of this confusion makes the plight of Ouray's biographer a hard one. However, I shall try to unravel some of the inconsistencies. If there are two conflicting accounts, I have tried to pick the one that makes the most sense, or I have given both. In the process, I shall also try to resolve questions such as whether Ouray sold out his people for a few beads and other trinkets, or whether he was a farsighted prophet who attempted to try to make the best deals possible for his people. To some extent this requires judgments about the Ute people. I am not Indian and I do not presume to look into their hearts. If I have written anything that offends, I apologize in advance. The truth about Ouray probably lies in between the extremes.

Ouray was a proud and powerful chief, as this photograph, taken shortly before his death in 1880, reveals. The lovely Chipeta was his constant companion and often his only confidant. At the time of this picture, Ouray was beginning to give up the white man's dress, retaining only his practical boots. Ouray was both mentally and physically sick at the time; his health was deteriorating from Bright's disease, but, perhaps even more importantly, his spirit was broken as well. The white man had lied to and cheated him, and now he was being asked to explain to his people why they must leave their homeland. Ouray and Chipeta must have discussed the situation often at that time. If only we could hear those words—would they have praised the white man or cursed him? (Denver Public Library)

Chapter One

THE UTES— THE BLUE SKY PEOPLE

To fully appreciate Chief Ouray, it is helpful to have an understanding of the Ute people as a whole, and to gain some idea of their heritage and traditions. Although there is some question as to the Utes early ancestry, several scholars presume to trace them back almost 10,000 years through the Paiutes of the Utah desert. It is generally agreed by these writers that the Paiutes came into that area from the north, and many authorities believe that some of those Indians may have continued south to become the Aztecs in Mexico. The Utes and the Paiutes both have Shoshonean ancestry and their language is Uto-Aztecan.

Another theory of early day Ute ancestry is that the Anasazi, the Navajo word for "ancient ones," were the forefathers of the Utes, yet it is also possible that the Anasazi were a separate tribe that abandoned their cliff palaces because of attacks by the Utes. For whichever reason, the Anasazi pueblos were vacant in the Four Corners region by 1300 A.D., which is the exact time the Utes were first recognized as a separate and distinct tribe in the area. Ute legend indicates that they have always occupied their land.

Almost as soon as they arrived in the Colorado-Utah area, the Utes were pushed into the mountains by pressure from the stronger and more established Plains Indians, and were probably the first Indians to live and travel extensively in what are now the Colorado mountains. They also had to contend with (but were generally allied with) the Navajos and Apaches to the south and the Shoshone and Snakes to the west. But once in the mountains, the Utes were in their element, and they defended their new territory savagely and successfully time and time again.

The very early Utes had no permanent homes, but rather roamed on foot in small bands of five to ten. They originally lived in caves or crude brush wickiups, moving about in an area that stretched from west central New Mexico to Wyoming, and from the edge of the eastern Colorado plains to the central Utah desert. But always their favorite summer habitat was in the central mountain parks of Colorado.

They were called Utahs or Yutas, and many variations of these names. But perhaps the most romantic of all was the name later given to them by the white men—"The Blue Sky People." The Utes referred to themselves simply as the people or ones who speak clearly.

Only an estimate can be made of the total Ute population because they had little political or social structure and a highly nomadic and independent nature. But their numbers were small, probably never over ten thousand and possibly as low as 3,500. The official U.S. government report of 1886 gave a figure of 3,391.

Although these early Utes hunted deer, elk and buffalo, it was the lowly jackrabbit that provided most of their food, clothing and blankets. Individual Ute groups needed plenty of room to hunt because it took a large area of the mountains to support even a small number of people. Each band of Utes had its own hunting territory, and other Utes would not intrude without first meeting to talk the situation over. They often lived a miserable existence, sometimes barely surviving from day to day. When they couldn't find deer or elk, they often ate roots, nuts, berries or even grasshoppers and mice to get through a harsh winter. They would use large dogs to pull travois filled with their possessions as they traveled constantly in search of food.

This diorama from the Ute Indian Museum at Montrose, Colorado, represents a typical Ute scene at any time between 1300 A.D. and 1650 A.D., when the Utes first gained the horse. The women at the right are grinding corn, while the men at the left are making weapons. The Utes were primarily hunters, but the squaws did sometimes plant little corn patches in the creek bottoms, leaving the cultivating and watering to the Great Spirit. If a crop developed, the grain was ground into a meal from which was made a tortilla-like bread that added variety to their main diet of meat and fish. The women also gathered fruits in season, some of which were dried for later use. (Colorado Historical Society)

Before acquiring the horse, the Utes were among the most impoverished of all the Indian tribes, often at the mercy of the larger and more powerful ones. After they obtained horses, the tables were turned, and the Utes became strong and feared. They also grew more successful at providing for themselves because they could roam farther than in the past and could raid other tribes, taking as spoils whatever they found useful. The wealth of a Ute brave was measured, in large part, by the number of horses he owned. At about the same time they acquired the horse, the Utes were also able to get rifles and ammunition from the Spanish settlements to the south. This allowed them to defend their mountains time and time again against other tribes. (Colorado Historical Society)

Late in the fall, they would move out of the mountains and come together at lower elevations for the winter months. Winter was a season for great social occasions. It was also the usual time for marriages to be contracted. In the early spring, the band would hold the Bear Dance, which was a four-day festival that was the most ancient and typical of all the Utes' dances. Afterwards, each family unit would prepare to go its separate way into the mountains for the summer.

Physically, the Utes were generally round, smooth-faced and stocky, even somewhat fat. Many were very dark skinned—in fact, so dark that some of the other Indian tribes disdainfully called the Utes the "Black Indians" or the "Black Faces." The average Ute was only about five feet five inches tall, making the Utes the shortest of all the Colorado Indian tribes. However, these descriptions are only generalities. There was a great deal of variance in individual appearance: some were tall, some were light-colored, and some even had beards.

About the middle of the 17th century, the hard life of the Utes changed dramatically when they obtained horses from the Spaniards. Because of the Utes proximity to Santa Fe and Taos, many historians feel that they were one of the first, if not the first, groups of Indians to obtain the horse. Wild horse bands multiplied rapidly, and the Utes increased their herds even faster by stealing from the Spaniards. By 1700, the Utes had acquired enough horses to allow them to trade with the Shoshone and other tribes to the north.

The Utes now could live in larger numbers. The family unit continued to be the basic unit of society, but Ute leaders began to appear who directed activities such as hunts and war parties. The Utes became aggressive and warlike because it was easier to steal livestock in New Mexico than it was to hunt wild game. The Utes began to move out of the mountains to raid other Indian or white villages.

The Ute Nation as a whole was transformed by the horse. It became an integral part of Ute culture, a symbol of power and influence, the Ute's most important single possession. A brave was judged by his horsemanship, and his inheritance in terms of horses. A man obtained a wife or not depending on the number of horses he owned.

In addition to the horse, the fact that the Spanish were moving into Ute territory helped improve the Ute way of life. Santa Fe was established in 1609, giving the Utes a source of trade. They had an abundance of hides to trade and found good use for the implements, clothes, horses, beads and ornamental goods they received in return.

Not only did the Utes raid the Spanish, but the Spanish made raids on the Utes periodically. For example, in 1637, Governor Luis de Rosas captured eighty Utes, whom he held for slaves, putting them to work as weavers, tanners or sheepherders. In the 1670s, the Spanish arranged a peace treaty with the Utes, but the Utes paid little heed to the treaty and attacked the northern Spanish outposts and the Navajos well into the middle of the 18th century.

Eventually the Utes lost their warlike ways towards the Spanish and did whatever was possible to cultivate their friendship. They began to capture Navajo or Paiute children to trade to the Spanish for necessary goods. (Children were used because adults proved too resistive.) On occasion the Utes would even sell their own children. Often the Spanish released the slaves, or they escaped when they grew older and returned to their tribes. Therefore, it became common for Utes to speak at least some Spanish and to take on Spanish characteristics. The Spanish, on occasion, even sent Ute children to school.

The Utes came to depend on the Spanish heavily. They learned to trade for and use firearms as well as the bow and arrow. The metals brought by the white man were refashioned to make arrow points, knives and axes. The Utes traded for blankets, beads and bells. With the horses and arms they acquired, they ranged onto the eastern plains of Colorado and began to hunt the buffalo, which they used for food, shelter and dozens of other purposes. Since the horse could pull heavier loads than their dogs, the Utes were able to use hide-covered tepees as did the Plains Indians.

But the Plains Indians also started using the horse extensively. As a result, the Utes were constantly defending their territory or revenging attacks that had been made on them by the Kiowa, Arapaho, Cheyenne, Comanche and Sioux. All of the scattered bands of Utes would sometimes gather together to fight under a loose, unofficial confederation. During raids or retaliatory attacks, the small Ute bands of five to ten sometimes grew to several hundred people under the leadership of a single subchief. These large groups often had two chiefs, a war chief and a peace chief. The war chief was usually a young warrior, while the peace chief was often an older, wiser man who would be in charge at all times except during war. Some chiefs ruled absolutely, but others were mere figureheads and almost powerless. A Ute chief had to have wisdom as well as courage, and had to be kind to the weak and liberal with the unfortunate.

The chief retained his position for life, and, with the consent of the tribe, chose his successor. The leading men, or subchiefs of the tribe would meet and discuss any important matter that came up. The chiefs and subchiefs were usually careful to listen to public opinion, and every adult male was given a full opportunity to discuss the question at hand with the others present. Individual members of the tribe still had plenty of freedom. For example, anyone could lead a war party by simply informing his war chief. The men would assemble, the target and plan would be explained, and those who wanted would then follow the instigator. However, if the medicine man was consulted and held the signs and omens to be unfavorable, the attack would be called off. There were always many subchiefs who were constantly changing as the older subchiefs and the young men of the tribe struggled for power. The winner would take power but could hold it only as long as he could meet the demands and the needs of his followers.

Several chiefs tried to bring the entire Ute Nation together under one chief, but all failed. This was in part due to the fact the Utes might be considered a truly democratic nation. The tribe's desires were highly important, but the Utes were proud of their individual freedom. They seldom took orders from anyone, and consequently they were hardly ever united on any particular point.

By the late 18th century, the Ute Nation was generally divided into a loose confederation known as the Seven Nations and composed of seven major divisions. The Mouache band numbered a little less than five hundred and usually occupied present day southern Colorado in the San Luis Valley, the Eastern Slope of Colorado, and New Mexico almost to Santa Fe. They were the most nomadic of the tribes and roamed freely almost everywhere. The approximately five hundred Utes in the Capote band inhabited the San Luis Valley in present day Colorado and the region in New Mexico where the towns of Abiquiu, Chama and Tierra Amarilla are now located. The Weeminuche band occupied the valleys of the San Juan, Las Animas, La Plata and Mancos rivers in present southwestern Colorado, southeastern Utah and northern New Mexico from Tierra Amarilla to the Colorado River. They numbered about seven hundred. The Mouache, Capote and Weeminuche were also collectively called the "Southern Utes."

The Tabeguache or Uncompahgre Utes lived in the valleys of the Gunnison and Uncompahgre rivers in what is now west central Colorado. Their numbers were estimated all the way from five

This photograph, made in 1899, shows both the "modern" tepee and the older brush shelter of the Utes. Since the Indians moved around with the seasons to be near their food supply, they did not always build the more permanent structure, known as the wickiup, except, perhaps, when they were in winter camp and would stay more or less stationary for a few months. The women in this picture, including the little girl, are wearing the traditional hairstyles of the Ute women over centuries of time. Apparently, they were not vulnerable to fickle changes of dress or make-up, making modifications only out of necessity or practicality. (Colorado Historical Society)

hundred to fifteen hundred, but they were definitely the largest of the Ute bands.

The Grand River Utes (also called the Parianuc) lived along the Grand River (now the Colorado River) in present day Colorado and

The seven Ute bands were never closely allied; therefore, some were more progressive than others. The Colorado Utes adapted the use of the tepee from their occasional contact with the Plains Indians. The Uintah band lived farther west in present day Utah and continued the use of shelters made of stick and brush for a longer period than the other Ute bands. In this picture, taken in the Uinta Valley, we do see a fine tepee. Nearer, in the foreground, is a brush shelter which is anchored to the base of the trees. The Ute lookout may be trying to catch a glimpse of game, or perhaps he is watching for the approach of a possible enemy. The tree platform could also be used to store supplies away from dogs and other animals. (Colorado Historical Society)

Utah and numbered about three hundred. The Yampa Utes inhabited the Yampa River Valley and adjacent land and numbered six or seven hundred. The Uintah Utes inhabited the Uintah Basin in present day Utah and numbered above five hundred. Collectively, the Grand, Yampa and Uintah were also called the "Northern Utes."

Until 1765, the Utes met the Spaniards on Spanish territory. In that year, the New Mexican Spanish governor, Cachupin, sent Juan Maria de Rivera to trade with the "Yutahs." He entered Colorado near present day Pagosa Springs, traveled west to the current site of Durango, went up the Dolores River and then across the Uncompahgre Plateau almost to the junction of the Uncompahgre and Gunnison rivers. Rivera then returned to New Mexico. Later he led three other expeditions into the area. In 1776, twenty-five days after the Declaration of Independence was signed in Philadelphia, Fray Silvestre Vélez de Escalante and Fray Atanasio Dominguez, along with twelve companions, traveled through the same area in an attempt to find an easier way to get from Santa Fe to California. In great part the route was chosen because of the known friendliness of the Utes. The Utes were not only amicable but they were very willing to act as guides. The Franciscan fathers noted that the wealthy Utes were mounted on horseback but that the poor ones didn't have horses and were living in huts instead of tepees. The party traveled a wandering course across Colorado and Utah. Some historians contend that this was due to the fact the Utes so loved the friars that they purposely made their trip longer.

Officially, the Spanish government continued to seek the Utes' friendship for trading purposes and as guides. However, from 1778 to near the end of the century, the Spanish prohibited private individuals from trading with the Utes. This action was supposedly to protect the Utes from being cheated but, in fact, was due to a desire of the crown to get any precious metals that were found. However, many trips were made that were not authorized and therefore not recorded. The Utes were quick to help open the area to the white man by showing him the easiest passes through the mountains or the quickest ways to cross the steep canyons and wide rivers. In some places, the Utes even built high stone monuments to show the direction of the trails, making it easy for the white man to follow. Almost every modern highway in the mountains of Colorado still traces an early day Ute trail.

While the Utes were usually friendly, the white man was unpredictable. The Utes were eager to share whatever food they had with the white man, but when the Utes asked for food, they were looked on as lowly beggars. At times the white man was friendly and brought gifts, but at other times he would shoot the Utes on sight. The Utes often joined the whites to fight common enemies, and they were of invaluable assistance in helping the whites conquer the Plains Indians. But then there were times when the white man made friends with the Utes' enemies! And the white man continued to encroach on Ute land. When there were only a few whites, they generally treated the Utes with respect and the Utes reciprocated. But as more and more Anglos came, they became more possessive and the Utes began to resist.

The Utes were especially alarmed when white settlers and soldiers began to appear on their land in the early 19th century. About this time, the fad of beaver hats caused the white man to travel into the mountains that he had so far generally avoided. Scores of trappers and traders moved into Ute territory. One of the earliest was Antoine Robideaux, a French trader from Missouri who established Ft. Uncompahgre near present day Delta, Colorado. Ft. Davy Crockett was established at about the same time in extreme northwest Colorado. Robideaux later established another fort on the Uinta River in eastern Utah.

The traders were a mixed blessing. They sometimes brought the Indians gifts, but they also killed the game. Sometimes they would intermarry with the Ute women. In 1821, Mexico gained its independence from Spain, and the new government continued friendly trade relations with the Utes. General Thomas James of the United States, while traveling in what is now New Mexico, wrote that in 1822 the Utes lived in comfortable houses and were

This exhibit in the Colorado Historical Society's museum at Montrose illustrates the soft, finely beaded buckskin clothing worn by the Utes and the hairstyles of both men and women. Most Ute males still wear the traditional two braids hanging forward over their shoulders. The Ute women usually wore their hair long and parted down the middle. Both men and women sometimes cropped their hair short, but quite often this was a sign of mourning. The Utes' buckskin was widely coveted by other tribes because of its softness and light color. The costumes shown here were probably those of a chief and his family; the average Ute's clothing was more practical. (Colorado Historical Society)

aggressive traders with the Spanish. He felt that both the Utes and their animals were far superior to the average Spaniard and reported that a Ute chief named Lechat came to him and spoke in fluent Spanish. Lechat said that he had come expressly to see

General James and wanted him to know that the Utes wanted the Americans trade. Lechat proposed:

"Come to our country with your goods. Come and trade with the Utahs. We have horses, mules and sheep, more than we want. We heard that you wanted beaver skins. The beavers in our country are eating up our corn. All our rivers are full of them. Their dams back up the water in the rivers all along their course from the mountains to the Big Water. Come over among us and you shall have as many beaver skins as you want." Turning round and pointing to the Spaniards, in most contemptuous manner and with a scornful look, he said, "What can you get from these? They have nothing to trade with you. They have nothing but a few poor horses and mules, a little puncha, and a little tola (tobacco and corn meal porridge) not fit for anybody to use. They are poor - too poor for you to trade with. Come among the Utahs if you wish to trade with profit. Look at our horses here. Have the Spaniards any such horses? No, they are too poor. Such as these we have in our country by the thousand and also cattle, sheep and mules. These Spaniards," said he, turning and pointing his finger at them in a style of contempt which John Randolph would have envied, "What are they? What have they? They won't even give us two loads of powder and lead for a beaver skin, and for a good reason, they have not as much as they want themselves. They have nothing that you want. We have everything that they have, and many things that they have not."

Although life for the Utes may not have been quite as easy as Lechat suggested, the Utes had risen to the peak of their prosperity. Because of the abundant game, fish, Mexican stock, and wild berries, the necessities of food and shelter were coming easy. The Utes had time to spend on less demanding activities such as family, religion and horse racing. Dancing, music and other artistic endeavors became a part of their life.

On a typical Ute day the women would make the fires soon after daybreak, gather water and cook the morning meal. The young boys would generally watch and care for the animals. The men might hunt, train the young boys, make war on another band, or participate in a religious ceremony. The women would tan hides, dry meat, make pemmican (dried and pounded meat, fruits and berries), make clothes, gather firewood and water, or search for berries and roots. The women might paint dancing or hunting scenes on rocks or hides. Or they might make baskets, covering some with piñon pitch to make them waterproof.

Ute beadwork was especially beautiful, often made of yellow, light green and light blue beads, and porcupine quills. The white

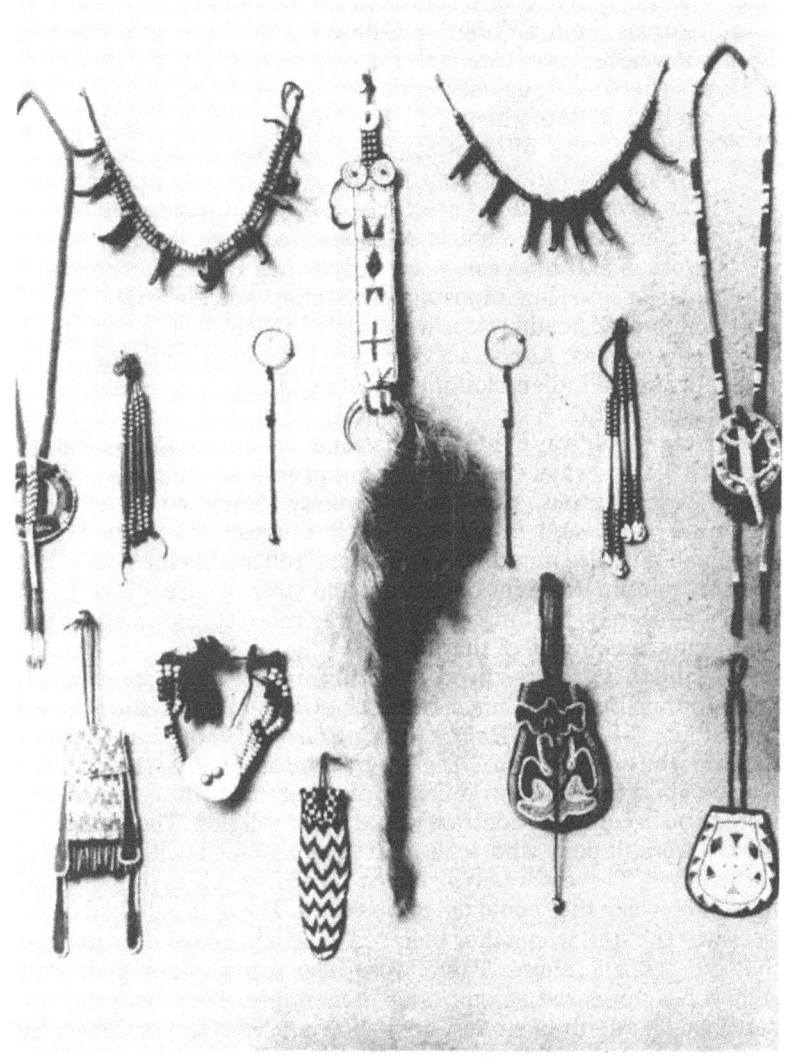

The Utes did not engage in pottery making or basket weaving to the extent of some of the other tribes in the Southwest. They did, however, excel in making utility leather articles and were skilled in the artistic ornamentation of such. These items included moccasins, pouches and jewelry. They did beautiful work with glass beads obtained from traders, as well as with the more traditional juniper seeds, porcupine quills and feathers. The small pouches at the bottom of the photo could have carried any number of items, including fetishes, which were small carvings of whatever game animal was being hunted. The Utes believed these brought them good luck. Bear claws ornament the upper necklaces; in the center a scalp dangles from what was probably a decoration for a lance or spear. (Denver Public Library)

man's beads, robes, bright cloth and ribbons were also integrated into Ute dress. LeRoy Hafen, in **Colorado, The Story of a Western Commonwealth**, describes well the details of the Utes' dress:

> The women usually wore loose, leather gowns .... belted at the waist ..... The dresses of the older women were often worn, patched, and black with grease and dirt; but those of the younger ones and of the wives of chiefs were clean, white and handsome.
>
> The men wore shirts or robes, leggings, breechclothes and moccasins. In early times they used no hats or caps; but imposing war bonnets and elaborate, feathered headdresses were worn in their dances and ceremonies. As contact with the whites increased, the primitive Indian clothing gave way in favor of white man attire.

Although their way of life became somewhat more sophisticated, the Utes were always moved by strong primitive emotions such as vanity, superstition, revenge or cruelty. They could also be generous, loyal and brave, but their dispositions were highly changeable. A Ute might laugh, joke and tell stories for hours, but the next minute he might be reticent and stoic. Above all the Ute's word was sacred. Nothing to the Ute was more shocking about the white man than the fact that he lied!

The land that the Utes lived in is still some of the most beautiful, dramatic and bountiful in America. The Utes called it "the Shining Mountains." It was a "Happy Hunting Ground," but it was a land that the white man was to desecrate by wantonly killing the game or tearing apart the land by mining or plowing. The white man's acts were to be in complete contrast with the Ute religion. The Utes were nature worshippers who took and were satisfied with whatever nature gave. There were many forces of nature such as thunder and lightning which they could not understand. The supreme god of the Utes was the sun, whom they believed to be a bisexual (he-she) god that created all things. There were also many minor gods that sometimes appeared as spirits or as animals. They believed the earth was made from stones, dirt, snow and rain thrown down by their god from the sky above. To the Utes, the earth was a living thing. A Ute could even hear the heartbeat of the world if he placed his ear against a certain rock on Uncompahgre Peak. It was a fine time to be born a Ute.

On September 1, 1913, in the Garden of the Gods near Colorado Springs, a band of Utes performed for a photographer the entire procedure for erecting a tepee. The five photographs shown here are selected from some two dozen that were made. The first step was to tie four poles together. These were then raised and crossed at the top to form the basic structure. The Ute male may have been a mighty warrior, hunter and sportsman; but when not engaged in these pursuits, he liked to lie around in the shade. Raising the tepee was women's work, and no self-respecting Ute male would lower himself to help. (Denver Public Library)

Most people have probably never thought about how the outer portion of the tepee got spread around the poles: the covering was attached to the end of a pole and raised so that it could lean against the crossed tops of the standing poles. The covering was made of hides sewn together with animal sinew into a semi-circular shape. A typical tepee took twelve elk hides (or fewer if made of Buffalo). Later, the United States government furnished canvas and thread to the Utes, since the buffalo and other large animals had been pretty well killed off. (Denver Public Library)

Small lodgepole pine trees were the favorite material for use in constructing the tepee, and they were found in abundance on the eastern slope of the Rocky Mountains. They were straight, mostly free of limbs, and light enough that they could be carried by horses. In building a tepee, the Indians continued to lean more poles against the originals until there was a total of twelve. The canvas or hide was then wrapped around all. Next, the bottoms of the poles were spread out in order to stretch the covering tight. In this picture, a Ute drum, made of a stretched hide, lies in front of the tepee. Several other tepees in the background have been completed already. (Denver Public Library)

The smoke hole (seen at the top left of this photograph) was adjustable. Two poles were inserted outside the tepee into pockets constructed for the smoke hole. They could then be moved so as to open the hole wider in warm weather or to close it down to a very small size in cold weather. The door flaps were adjustable in the same way. Many tepees had a simple ornamental design such as this one, which is a different color at the bottom. Sometimes, figures of men or animals were painted on the outside of the covering to record some important event. (Denver Public Library)

The bottom edge of the covering was then either staked with pegs or weighted down with stones. The tepee could easily shelter the average Ute family of five or six and was reasonably warm in winter when a small fire was built on the inside. The tepee had the advantage of being extremely portable and easy to assemble. The pieces could be disassembled and bundled up, as shown in the foreground of this photograph. The tepee could then be transported to its next location without the Utes having to worry about finding materials for shelter at their new site. (Denver Public Library)

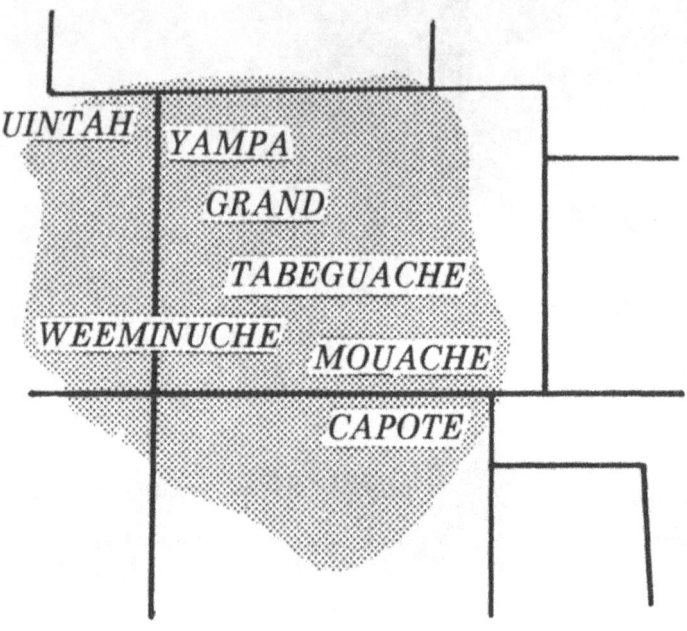

UTE DOMAIN ABOUT 1830

Before the white man invaded their territory, the Utes ranged throughout the eastern half of present day Utah, the northern half of New Mexico, and most of Colorado. The shaded portion of this map represents the area they occupied almost constantly at about the time that Ouray was born. However, when hunting or engaged in warfare, there were times when the Utes often ranged hundreds of miles farther away. The location of each of the seven bands is only approximate since they constantly roamed. The Utes wouldn't hesitate to go into each other's territory as long as the purpose was friendly, and they quite often intermarried.

The Ute Indians lived in the beautiful, but rugged, Rocky Mountains of Colorado, which they called "The Shining Mountains." It was a land of primitive, rugged beauty; an area of plentiful game and a variety of edible fruits, berries and other plants. The large mountain parks contained elk and deer, and in the summer, millions of buffalo fed on the long, nutritious grass that also made the Ute horses faster than those of their enemies. The steep mountains and deep gorges also served to protect the Utes from enemy tribes. (Bill Fries III)

Chapter Two

THE EARLY YEARS—
NEW MEXICO

Not too much is known of Ouray's early years, and what is known is often contradicted. Most authorities agree that he was born in 1833, somewhere in the valley between Taos and Abiquiu, New Mexico. The Old Spanish Trail ran for hundreds of miles through Ute territory from Santa Fe or Taos, through Abiquiu (which was about the same size as Taos), and then on to Los Angeles on the Pacific Coast. The trail was used extensively by both the Utes and the fur traders. This route was used rather than a more direct route to California because it avoided the unfriendly Apaches and Navajos, allowed the travelers to stay among the friendly Utes, and was far enough north to allow adequate (although sparse) grazing and water for the animals. The traffic over the trail hit its peak from 1830 to 1848. The favorite commodities carried over the trail were the woolen blankets and coats of the Santa Fe area, which were exchanged for horses, slaves and mules for the return trip.

The Abiquiu-Taos area had already been populated by the Spanish for over two hundred years at the time Ouray was born. Its population of about three thousand was a mixture of rich and poor, priests and sinners, free men and slaves. The area was a melting pot of Indians, Anglos and Mexicans. Every year in Taos, fairs were held to which all the Indians came. There they traded horses, hides and other surpluses the tribes might have. It was a wild time and a wild place, and, prophetically, the year of Ouray's birth was a time of intense meteorite activity—on the night of November 13, 1833, over 200,000 shooting stars appeared, illuminating the earth. For years afterwards, that year was called "The Year of the Shooting Stars."

Ouray was born the son of a Jicarilla Apache father and a Tabeguache Ute mother. It was normal for a Ute to become a member of the woman's tribe, so both Ouray's father and Ouray became Tabeguache. The members of Ouray's tribe were in the habit of spending much of their time in the Taos Valley and San Luis Park, and along the Sangre de Cristo Mountains. In that region they were accustomed to meeting the Apaches, who came up from the south. It was even very common for the women of one band of Indians to marry out of their tribe.

Ouray's father was named Guera Murah, but was sometimes called Salvador. Guera Murah had been stolen from the Apaches by the Utes when he was very young and raised as a Ute. It was not unusual for warring bands of Indians to steal the women and children of other tribes. The children were adopted and raised as if they were the natural children of their "foster parents." Guera Murah was given complete freedom and all of the privileges of the tribe, and he soon rose to the rank of a minor chief. Nevertheless some of the Utes still, on occasion, called him "the Apache"—curse words for the Utes.

Because the Utes had no written language, Ouray's name was to be spelled many different ways throughout the years—Ura, Ourai, Uri, Ure and Ou-Ray, to name but a few of the variations. Finally he settled on the spelling "Ouray," and many years later, when Ouray learned to write his own name, he preferred this spelling. The Utes themselves later called their chief "Oolay" or "Ulay" because they had trouble pronouncing their r's. While most authorities agree that Ouray's name means "the arrow" in English, Ouray in later life is supposed to have told Major James B. Thompson of the Denver Ute Agency that the name had no meaning. He said that "Ooay" was the first word he spoke as a child, so that was what his parents called him.

Ouray was raised in a Spanish atmosphere. For the time, and considering that he was an Indian, he received a rather decent education from the Catholic friars in Taos. He often attended mass, although he was not a member of the Catholic Church. Ouray's father and mother became so accustomed to the Spanish ways that they were supposedly married and given white man's or Christian names in a little adobe church at the Red River crossing, and even had Ouray baptized there. He spent much of his preteen years working at a hacienda near Taos.

Because of his Catholic upbringing, Ouray found it easy in later life to partially convert to Christianity. But he only used Christianity as a supplement to the Ute religion. He is claimed to have once said that "if one religion is good, two religions are much better." Ouray grew up without drinking or smoking, and he refrained from these habits for the rest of his life. Since his family lived near Abiquiu and away from the main tribe, it was not until adolescence that Ouray learned many of the Ute ways. Spanish was the native language of New Mexico, and it became Ouray's preferred language. Ouray said that he "thought" in Spanish. By the time he was eighteen, Ouray spoke at least some English, Spanish, Ute and Apache, as well as being proficient in Indian sign language. More importantly, he had some understanding of the customs and teachings of each of these cultures.

Several years after Ouray was born, his mother had another son who was named Quenche. But tragedy struck—Ouray's mother died shortly after Quenche's birth. Ouray and his brother were raised by other women of the tribe who were in the area. In the mid-

1840s, Guera Murah remarried, and in 1845 Ouray's half sister Susan was born. A few years later Ouray and Quenche were left with a Spanish couple while their parents (who supposedly never really liked the Taos area) went to the Western Slope of Colorado to be with the rest of the tribe. Eventually Ouray's parents had another daughter and two brothers, but the brothers died young. White traders such as Phillip Thompson and William Craig, who established Ft. Davy Crockett on the Green River in 1837, and trader Antoine Robideaux, who established Ft. Uncompahgre near the present day Delta, Colorado, had recently been run off by the Indians. Fort Uncompahgre had even been burned. This created a critical situation for the Northern Utes, who needed someone who had trading experience with the whites to fill the void. Guera Murah was expected to help reestablish this trading relationship.

The Spanish family that Ouray and Quenche were left with were quite wealthy for the time and for the place. Ouray was able to live a considerably better life than many Utes or even most Spaniards. He spent quite a bit of his time taking care of the Spaniard's sheep herd, gathering firewood and doing other domestic chores. Ouray began to dress and act like the Spaniards.

The mid-1840s became a time of Ute upheaval in the northern New Mexico area, because Mexican land grants were using up much of the territory that the Utes needed for hunting. The Utes attacked many of the Mexican settlements in the Taos Valley and north of Espanola, and in 1843, they forced a group of Mexican farmers out of Antonito. The unrest continued. In 1844, the Capote Utes attacked Rio Arriba settlements probably in retaliation for a Ute killed by Governor Martinez de Lejanza, and in 1845, the Utes attacked the settlement of Ojo Caliente. Finally, in 1846, about sixty Ute chiefs went to Santa Fe to confer with Colonel Doniphan where they were induced to sign a treaty promising to remain peaceful.

In June, 1846, the Mexican-American war erupted. Ouray witnessed firsthand the awesome military power of the American troops. One of the earliest actions of the war occurred in Ouray's "backyard" when General Stephen W. Kearny and his "Army of

It is very likely that Ouray was carried like this by his mother when he was very young. For centuries the Ute cradle board allowed mothers to tend their children while continuing to do many of their regular chores. Most Indian tribes used the cradle board, but each tribe's way of decorating them was unique. Apparently, being so confined did not hurt the children, except that they often developed a flat spot on the back of their heads where their soft skulls rested against the hard backing of the board. (Colorado Historical Society)

the West" troops left Leavenworth, Kansas, stopped at Ft. Bent, swept over Raton Pass, captured Santa Fe on August 18, 1846, and set up a United States civil government in less than a week's time on his push to California. The commandant of Santa Fe, Governor Arriyo, offered little resistance. Charles Bent, one of the owners of Ft. Bent, was made American governor. Ouray witnessed and was evidently impressed with the large number of United States troops and their cannons, rifles and other equipment. Although the army was scattered, it totaled 1,600 men, 1,500 wagons, 15,000 oxen and 1,000 mules. In July of 1846, all of New Mexico and that part of Colorado not included in the Louisiana Purchase became United States territory.

The Americans immediately went to work to make sure the Utes remained peaceful. Within a month, General Kearny took steps to contact the Utes of the southern Colorado region, and sent Major William Gilpin (later to become the first governor of Colorado) to visit the three Southern Ute tribes. On September 20, 1846, Gilpin returned to Santa Fe with a few Indians who met with General Kearny. Later in the month, Gilpin went with eighty-five men into the San Luis Valley and persuaded sixty of the principal Utes to come to Santa Fe. There they met Colonel Doniphan and agreed to remain peaceful. Later that year, an unofficial treaty was arranged with the Mouache Utes by Kit Carson and William Gilpin.

In 1847, Ouray again got to witness, or at least hear about, the military power of the United States. On January 19, fifteen hundred Mexicans and Pueblo Indians revolted against their new American masters at Taos. They attacked and killed fourteen Americans, including Governor Charles Bent, who was decapitated in front of his horrified wife and children. Colonel Sterling Price, with 350 troops and 130 volunteers, fought through a raging snowstorm from Santa Fe to the Taos Pueblo. The U.S. troops quickly quelled the rebellion, killing in retaliation over 150 Indians, with a loss of only seven soldiers. At the other end of Ute territory that same year, the Mormons expelled the Utes and moved into the Salt Lake City area.

On December 30, 1849, the first formal U.S. treaty was made with most of the Utes at Abiquiu, New Mexico. James S. Calhoun represented the United States as Indian agent. There were no boundaries set for the Utes by the treaty, which merely stated that the Utes would be allowed (and they promised to stay on) their "usual territory." The Utes recognized the sovereignty of the United States and agreed to remain at peace with them and allow the Americans safe passage through the Ute territory. The Utes were also to return any stolen property in their possession and allow captive Americans and Mexicans to go free. The Utes were to begin to settle down and devote themselves to agriculture. It is probable that the Utes didn't realize the significance of this last promise, because they fought against being submitted to that way of life for the next thirty years. In return the Utes were to receive a total of $5,000 in annuities each year. Twenty-nine chiefs were present to

The early day Spanish colonies in New Mexico functioned on a communal plan, with each village specializing in providing something essential to be used by the entire colony. Ranchos de Taos provided milk, butter, cheese and some meat. About four miles southwest of the town of Taos stands this old church, built 350 years ago to serve the colonists and some of the Indians in the immediate area. It is probable that Ouray, as a boy, received some religious instruction here since he was apprenticed to a Spanish family in the area. What little academic instruction he gained was probably under the tutelage of the priests or friars of this church. (Colorado Historical Society)

make the treaty. Chief Quiziachigiate of the Capote Utes signed as the principal chief. Nevava was one of the subchiefs present, and he was probably attended by Ouray's father and possibly Ouray himself.

The treaty further provided that the Utes pledge: "their existence, as a distinct tribe, to abstain, for all time to come, from all depredations; to cease the roving and rambling habits which have hitherto marked them as a people, to confine themselves strictly to the limits which may be assigned to them; and to support themselves by their own industry, aided and directed as it may be by the wisdom, justice and humanity of the American people." However the Utes didn't cease to roam—in fact, they became more nomadic and warlike as the whites continued to encroach by settling and hunting on their territory. In 1842 and again in 1848, John C. Fremont had attempted to cross the San Juans in the heart of Ute territory. White trappers had been invading the territory for several decades, and the Mexican ranchers were continuing to push up from the south. As a result, the Utes began to obtain arms from the Mormons at Salt Lake. It looked like the time was coming when the Indian would strike back at the white man.

By the year 1850, Ouray had grown to adulthood. Physically he was about five feet, seven inches tall, stout yet strong. His head was large, and he always wore his hair long and braided to lay on each side of his chest. His early childhood had made him more than just an ordinary Ute. Because of their proximity to the Spaniards and other white men, and because the Southern Utes obtained the horse before the other Utes, it is generally agreed that they progressed towards civilization faster than the other Ute bands. Many of the Northern Utes did not even see a white man for another decade or two. Ouray had become a very unique Ute with a keen awareness and understanding of the Spanish, Ute and Anglo cultures which were all merging during his lifetime in the Southwest. It could even be said that Ouray had become a man of many worlds and many cultures. He was already armed to do verbal battle with the whites. His grasp of the political, social and military situations of the time was far greater than those of his fellow Indian. He had accepted the fact that the white man had superior weapons and far greater numbers. He realized that although the Utes might win a small battle, there was no way they would ever win a war against the whites. And yet his knowledge was a two-sided sword. Because he had not been raised as a Ute, Ouray may not have been able to fully understand and appreciate the heritage of his own people.

Although the woman in the photograph is identified as "Chipeta, Ouray's Squaw," most authorities agree that this is a picture of Susan, his younger sister. As a child, Susan was captured and almost killed by the Arapahos before she was saved by passing white soldiers. In later life, she was married to a White River Ute, and she befriended and protected the three white women and two children who were held captive by that tribe following the Meeker Massacre. Because of her kindness, this picture was widely circulated. The earliest known copy is credited to Chamberlain, although it was later sold under the name of W.H. Jackson. Note the U.S. Army belt buckle and numerous Navajo bracelets she is wearing. (Denver Public Library)

The square at Taos village, three miles from the Taos pueblo (which is the largest pueblo in what is now the state of New Mexico), was a trading and social center for the ranchers and farmers in the vicinity. In 1847, the Pueblo Indians revolted against the United States, killing the local governor, Charles Bent, as well as thirteen other Americans. United States soldiers later retaliated, killing over 150 Indians. Ouray was living in the area, and although he was only fourteen, he must have seen or heard of the awesome American military power. (Colorado Historical Society)

Kit Carson, the famous scout and frontiersman, had his home in Taos from 1843 to 1863. The house, on the left in the photograph, was built in 1825 and still exists as a museum. Carson met with many different Indians in his home, including Chief Ouray. He was particularly good friends with the Utes and could speak their language fluently. In 1853, he was officially appointed their agent, and he held this position until 1859. He often counseled Chief Ouray about how the Utes should deal with the white man. (Colorado Historical Society)

Chapter Three

THE TABEGUACHE— OURAY'S RISE TO POWER

In 1850, Ouray, at the age of seventeen, gave up his life as a sheepherder and moved to western Colorado. His father, even though Apache, had become a leader of the Tabeguache band of Utes. Ouray wished to become a full member of the tribe and to learn more of his people's culture. For the next decade, he was to enjoy the simple ways of the Utes, learning to love the awe-inspiring mountains and desert of the Ute territory. He decided not to return to Taos; the area in which he was living, the Uncompahgre Plateau, was the heart of Ute territory.

In 1850, shortly after Ouray went to the Tabeguache Ute country, his father died. Pursuant to Ute custom, Ouray and his brother each inherited a dozen ponies. Soon thereafter, at the age of seventeen, Ouray was belatedly initiated into adulthood by the Ute puberty rite that a young Ute male usually went through at age fourteen or fifteen. He was smeared with the blood of a mountain lion, which was supposed to make him strong and cunning, and he spent the night with a young Indian girl. His training as a warrior now began, and the Utes considered him to be an adult for all purposes.

In 1849, gold had been discovered in California. The Utes' condition began to change radically in the early 1850s as the white man arrived in their territory. In 1850, the United States opened an Indian agency near Taos with John Greiner as agent. The Utes were becoming poorer and they needed the white man's presents. The first agency was a failure and soon closed for lack of funds. However, it reopened in 1853 with Kit Carson as the agent. Carson held the position until 1859 and probably understood the Utes better than any white man of his time. He and Ouray were to become good friends. The Indians respected Carson; he was sympathetic to their problems and absolutely fair with them. He could speak the Ute language fluently and had adapted himself to the Indian way of life.

In 1853 Captain John W. Gunnison mapped a great portion of the Ute territory while exploring for a route for the transcontinental railroad. The party traveled the same trail that had been followed earlier that year by John C. Fremont as he went over the Continental Divide at Cochetopa or Saguache Pass, down Tomichi Creek and the Gunnison River to the Black Canyon of the Gunnison, over Blue Mesa to the Uncompahgre River near present day Montrose, and down the Uncompahgre, Gunnison and Colorado

Christopher "Kit" Carson had this picture taken in his middle years, about the time he was deeply involved with the Utes. Although he ceased to be an official Indian agent in 1861, Carson was a good friend of Chief Ouray and had a major part in the United States treaty negotiations of 1863 and 1868. Carson had adapted himself to the Indian way of life and understood well their point of view. He even fought in some of the wars that the Indians had against each other. Although he was a small man, he was a prized scout and a ferocious fighter. It was Carson who helped Ouray realize that it was hopeless for the Utes to fight the whites and that he needed to be skillful at the bargaining table instead of the battlefield. (Colorado Historical Society)

rivers into Utah. Although they saw few Indians at first, they were followed almost constantly from the time they reached the Black Canyon area. Jacob H. Schiel, geologist and surgeon for the Gunnison party, later wrote of the party's meeting with a Tabeguache band of Utes (of which Ouray might have been a part):

> They were for the most part well clothed and did not have at all the famished, degenerate appearance of many of the prairie tribes. A certain prosperity seemed to be the general rule among them. Their warriors were powerfully built, of medium height with broad, high chests but their legs had the usual bowlegged shape of all Indian legs. Their faces maintained a very ugly expression because of the great width of the base of their noses. The speech which they addressed to us at first was overbearing, almost threatening, and they made it very clear that if we did not give them presents they would take them .... The chief made a long speech in which he assured us that the Utahs had always been the best friends of the Americans. He commended us urgently to ask the White Father, when we returned to him, to send yearly presents to the Utahs, too, as he did the other tribes through whose lands his white children go. This was promised him, of course. Peace was concluded, the pipe was smoked, and the next morning the chiefs were summoned to receive some presents.

The trail followed by Gunnison (and first used by Robideaux and later Fremont) became a widely used route for parties traveling from Missouri to California. It tied in with the Old Spanish Trail shortly after crossing into present day Utah.

In 1853, Indian agent Michael Steck reported that the Utes were beginning to feel the scarcity of game in the traditional Ute territory, and that, additionally, they were being attacked by the Plains Indians when they ventured onto the Plains to try to hunt buffalo. The United States distributed rations to the Mouaches and Capotes in 1852 at Abiquiu and in 1853 did the same at Arroyo Hondo, Red River and near Chama in New Mexico.

Although the Utes' condition was declining, it was a happy time for Ouray. About 1853, Ouray married a Tabeguache maiden, Black Mare. He had met her a short time earlier at the annual Bear Dance, which was a three or four day Ute celebration held in March of each year to celebrate the coming of spring. The Utes believed that the first thunder of spring awakened the bear from his winter's hibernation and the dance in turn would also awaken the Utes for their hunting.

The Bear Dance was a mating dance. The scattered bands would come together, often bringing members of other tribes, and would build an "avinkwep" or "cave of sticks." A circular enclosure was swept clean and a "fence" of brush boughs and leaves formed the dance floor. The huge dance area always had a large door facing southwest (since the bear always chooses a den into which the sun will shine during some part of the day). Drums and moraches (notched sticks rubbed with another stick) were played. Everyone wore their best clothing. Women paired off with the men of their choice during the dance. Dancing started slowly, as the bears were groggy. The women would form one line and the men another. Gradually the pace would pick up as songs were sung and dances were had. It was a mixture of religion, matchmaking and a great communal feast. Then gradually the gathering would break up as hunting parties would leave for the early spring hunts at higher elevations.

Marriage was a rather casual affair among the Utes, and polygamy (by either sex) was allowed, although not common. Cohabitation might better describe the Ute custom rather than marriage, because there was no real commitment to continue the relationship for life. More than likely Black Mare was courted in the usual Ute way, which consisted of Ouray singing and possibly playing his flute to her from behind the bushes near her tepee. If she wanted him to come to her tent that night, she would throw a few pebbles in his direction. Her parents would share the tent with her and her lover that night. The marriage ritual consisted of the male dressing up in his finest and killing a deer or elk, which he left by his intended wife's tepee. The woman would also dress up and go to the animal, squealing in fake surprise when she saw it. The animal was dressed by the woman and taken back to the lodge, where a stew was made. The man arrived at the tepee and ate the stew while the woman undressed. Ouray could have also run his horse in front of her tepee and given her family sheep, horses or cattle. From this time on, they would be considered to be married.

Divorce was far less complicated than marriage: men and women were equal in marriage or divorce. If only one party desired such, that party merely threw the other's possessions out of the tepee.

In October of 1854, the Utes met with the Superintendent of Indian Affairs, David Meriwether. Kit Carson had rounded up the Utes and reported:

> On their way to their hunting grounds, the smallpox broke out among them. The leading men of the band of Mouache Utahs died. They came to the conclusion that the Superintendent was the cause of the disease being among them, that he had collected them for the purpose of injuring (them), that to the head man he gave each a blanket coat, and that every one that received a coat died. That the coats were the cause of the deaths the Indians firmly believed and the murderer of the Indians being allowed to escape unpunished and they having but poor faith in anything the Superintendent promised them, they com-

menced preparing for war. Joined the Apaches and commenced committing depredations. They attacked the settlement of (the) Costilla, killed some men and drove off nearly all the stock, and stole and murdered citizens as they be found.

In 1854 and 1855, the Utes and Jicarilla Apaches began menacing the white settlers of southern Colorado. Then, on December 25, 1854, the Fort Pueblo Massacre occurred. The Indians again believed that they had been purposely infected with smallpox. Chief Tierra Blanco of the Mouache Utes, together with Jicarilla Apaches, led the raid on Pueblo. Most of the Indians were Mouaches. All fifteen white male inhabitants of the fort (soldiers, Mexicans and traders) were killed and two boys and a woman were taken captive. During the next year, several ranchers were killed or driven out.

In the meantime, the Indians also realized that actual war was on, so they turned to the San Luis Valley and attacked the little settlements there. Several men were killed, and cattle and sheep were

The Ute Bear Dance was a three- or four-day social function held in the early spring. The scattered tribes would come together, and the young people would have a chance to meet. This dance was unique to the Utes but was later copied by other tribes. A large dance floor was made by enclosing an area of ground with a circular wall or fence of sticks. The dancing took place inside the circle, with the men and women each forming their own lines and facing each other. The basic rhythm was two large steps forward, then three small steps backward, with the lines moving in unison. Ouray met his first wife, Black Mare, at the Bear Dance of 1853. The celebration is still held today, and the Utes allow, and even encourage, whites to watch. (Colorado Historical Society)

driven off. Even the garrison at Fort Massachusetts was endangered. The commander took the precautions of cutting all the trees and brush about the fort, moving the haystacks nearer the fort, throwing up breastworks about the blockhouse, and ensuring that sentinels kept a tireless watch. The Utes decided not to attack.

The Utes often played a flute-like instrument as part of their courting ritual. It is therefore very possible that Ouray used this device while courting Black Mare, although nothing is really known about his musical talents. His innate goodness and fine personality probably held the greater attraction for her. Flutes were made of split red cedar, which was hollowed out, then put back together with thongs. This particular Ute also has bells on leather straps wrapped around his ankles to add to the music. Another courting ritual Ouray probably participated in was to leave a freshly killed deer at Black Mare's tepee. Once she had dressed it and had invited him to her tepee, they were in effect married. (Denver Public Library)

The whites began an aggressive campaign to suppress Chief Blanco and his Southern Ute Indians. In early March, 1855, five hundred soldiers under Colonel T.T. Fauntleroy, along with four companies of volunteers under Colonel Ceran St. Vrain, left Taos with Kit Carson as a guide and started pursuing the Utes into Colorado, defeating them badly and killing about forty Utes on March 19, 1855, near Saguache. They chased the fleeing Utes and defeated them in seven straight encounters. By July the Utes had asked for peace, resulting in a treaty being signed in Abiquiu in September, 1855. The treaty provided that the Mouache Utes were to give up their territory except for a 1,000 square mile reservation west of the Rio Grande and north of La Jara Creek. In return they were to receive $66,000. However, the treaty was not ratified by the U.S. Senate so it never took effect. The Utes were generally friendly with the whites from this time on. Ouray was twenty-two at the time.

According to some sources, Ouray's first act as a chief occurred about August, 1855, during one of the encounters the whites had with the Southern Utes. Shavano, Ouray's early good friend, had become a war chief for the Utes. When Kaneache of the Mouache Utes sent a runner to ask for help to fight the whites, Ouray refused to do so and held the messenger. Ouray believed that the white man's reprisals would far outnumber the few white men Kaneache might kill. Ouray then asked Shavano to send runners to warn Kit Carson, who was camped near Raton Pass. Shavano and Ouray rode to the little Spanish town of Guadalupe on the Conejos River and picked up about twenty warriors along the way. The group of Utes helped defend the whites, and Ouray wounded and captured Kaneache, but the rest of the Mouaches fled after about a dozen were killed. Later, after his wounds were healed, Kaneache was released by the whites.

In 1856, the Tabeguache Utes had a bad winter, and they were forced to go to Abiquiu to ask for food. On September 4, 1856, a meeting was held by Meriwether, Carson and the Utes at Abiquiu,

New Mexico. Presents were distributed, but one Indian chief was disappointed by receiving an old blanket and tried to attack Meriwether. Carson reported (after having a falling out himself with Meriwether):

> I cannot see how the Superintendent can expect Indians to depart satisfied .... They are given a meal by the Superintendent, then the presents are given. Some get a blanket; those that get none are given a knife or hatchet or some vermillion, a piece of red or blue cloth, some sugar, and perhaps a few more trinkets. They could more than earn the quantity they receive in one day's hunt, if left in their country. They could procure skins and furs and traders could furnish the same articles to them and they would be saved the necessity of coming such a distance, thereby not causing their animals to be fatigued and themselves have to travel without food. If presents are given them it should be taken to their country. They should not be allowed to come into the settlements, for every visit an Indian makes to a town it is of more or less injury to him.

Most of the period between 1856 and 1860 Ouray spent living a normal nomadic Ute life. He traveled widely while hunting, visiting other Utes, fishing, and fighting the Plains Indians, especially the Sioux and Arapaho. Five major Indian skirmishes occurred in the late 1850s and early 60s, and Ouray distinguished himself in all of these. In the late summer of 1856, Ouray proved his worth as a warrior when thirty-eight Arapaho and Cheyenne stole about forty Ute horses. Chief Nevava took ten warriors, including Ouray, Shavano and Colorow. Ouray suggested an ambush rather than a direct attact. The Utes killed eight of the enemy, regained the stolen horses and didn't lose a single man.

> Kaneache was a Mouache Ute war chief who was shot and captured by Ouray in 1855 when he threatened to attack white settlers. He was imprisoned for a while and carried a grudge against Ouray for the rest of his life. In later years, Kaneache was always quick to oppose whatever plan Ouray might have in mind. In 1880, when Ouray traveled to the Southern Utes to try to convince them to sign the treaty that would eventually force most of them to leave Colorado, Kaneache was, as usual, his major opponent. Ouray died before he could accomplish his task, but ironically Kaneache was struck by lightning several days later. Taking this as a sign that Ouray was right, the Utes finally signed the treaty. (Denver Public Library)

Ouray loved to sit around the campfires listening to the elders and learning as much as he could about the Ute ways. He would often travel to Conejos to take part in, or listen to, the head Utes' discussions on tribal matters. Ouray soon gained a reputation as an adept and ferocious warrior and hunter. He could ride, run, shoot or use a knife better than most of his band. Ouray loved to fight. He killed several Utes for Chief Nevava to enforce discipline within the tribe. No one wanted to cross Ouray. Once a year in the fall the Utes would travel to the eastern plains of Colorado to hunt buffalo for their winter supply of meat and robes. They would usually fight with the Plains Indians, and Ouray again continually distinguished himself.

In 1857, U.S. officials recommended that the Capote Utes and the Jicarilla Apaches be removed to the San Juan River Basin and made to become self-sufficient. The next year officials decided the Tabeguache Utes would be attached to the agency at Abiquiu. It was also noted that the Tabeguache were the largest band of Utes that year. Hostilities continued to break out between the Utes and Navajos. Eventually the Utes joined U.S. troops in 1859 and 1860 to wage war against the Navajos. The general feeling was that the Navajos had gone too far in their depredations on settlements and neighboring tribes and needed to be punished.

Ouray's first wife bore him a son about 1857, whom they named Queashegut. Ouray dearly loved the boy, who was to be his only child, and called him Paron or "apple," since, according to Ouray, he had two dimples and "a round face like an apple." The boy was also called Cotoan by his cousins. But that year tragedy struck— Black Mare died, some say of the childbirth and others say of a rattlesnake bite.

In 1859 Ouray married another Tabeguache maiden. Chipeta (which supposedly means "the charitable one" or "white singing bird") was sixteen (born June 10, 1843) and Ouray was twenty-six at the time of their marriage. Chipeta was a Kiowa Apache whose parents were both killed in a raid. She was found crawling around the deserted camp by the Utes. Because she was Kiowa, she did not have the typical female Ute woman features. Chipeta was beautiful, a tall slender woman with a very straight, sharp nose and well-defined features. She was supposedly appointed to watch Ouray's child after Black Mare died. There is a possibility that Chipeta was actually the stepsister of Black Mare and it was her duty to take over Ouray's household tasks. Although intelligent, she never learned to speak more than a few words of English. She was a typical Ute wife of the time: hard working, shy, quiet, and the person who did almost all of the day-to-day household tasks, which would have included tanning Ouray's deerskins and elkskins to use for sewing his clothes and moccasins; cooking, including preparing dried meats; hauling wood and carrying water.

Chipeta helped raise Paron and loved him as her own child. Ouray and Chipeta became inseparably devoted to each other.

Shavano was an early day friend of Ouray's who became a war chief for the Utes. He was the complete opposite of Kaneache and was always ready to help Ouray in any way possible. However, in later years his attitude may have changed; it was reported at the treaty conference of 1873 that he was "a man of some ability and for some years has been ambitious of usurping Ouray's position, and for some time since came near succeeding. He is a great drunkard and gambler and easily influenced by either money or whiskey." He is shown here with a Presidential Peace medal and, fittingly enough for a war chief, a revolver. (Colorado Historical Society)

On June 27, 1860, Lafayette Head was appointed Ute Indian agent at Conejos at the suggestion of Kit Carson. Head was an unusual man who left his native Illinois for Colorado to escape his neighbors' wrath when he married a twelve-year-old girl. When she died, he married a wealthy Spanish widow who lived near Conejos. He became a very powerful man in the area and later served as a representative to the New Mexico legislature. The Utes accused him of stealing their supplies and substituting spoiled provisions. Head evidently appointed Ouray to be his interpreter at a salary of $500 per year to help take some of the heat off his actions. (Colorado Historical Society)

Throughout the rest of their lives, they were constantly together whether at home or on a diplomatic journey to Washington. In fact, Ouray seemed to have no close male friends, preferring evidently to spend as much time alone with Chipeta as possible. This was unusual among the Utes, who considered women to be inferior to the men when it came to tribal matters.

In 1859, gold was discovered near Pike's Peak, and white men began to flood into the Ute territory. A story in the **Rocky Mountain News**, July 9, 1859, featured this headline: "Trouble with the Indians—Our miners shot and scalped by the Utah savages without provocation." There were many other reports of difficulties between the whites and Indians, and many exaggerated tales of murders and scalpings were reported by an unscrupulous press. A correspondent of the **Rocky Mountain News** wrote in November, 1859:

> While in Taos, New Mexico ... I was requested by Kit Carson, government Agent for the Ute Indians, to say to the Miners here, that he hoped to visit this region early next spring, with several leading 'braves' of the tribe, to conclude a permanent peace between them and the whites. He deems this very desirable, as the Utes are the most dangerous of the mountain Indians, excellent shots with the rifle, and if hostile, will be likely to destroy many small prospecting parties and solitary travelers next season.

In 1860, gold was also discovered in the San Juans of southwestern Colorado, although it would be a decade before any large scale development would take place. If they didn't strike it rich, many of the Pikes Peak gold miners stayed on and started farms. As the Utes' land was thus reduced, the tribe became poorer, and the U.S. government established several more supply posts to furnish them goods to help them through the winter.

By 1860, at the age of twenty-seven, Ouray had risen to the position of a subchief of the Tabeguache tribe. He was an "enforcer" for Nevava and was known to be so dangerous that only the most foolhardy challenged him. Kit Carson, who often talked with Ouray about Indian-white relations, suggested to him that the Utes seek a treaty to define a clear boundary to their territory. When Ouray passed the suggestion on to Chief Nevava, Nevava said there was no need for such a treaty, as everyone knew the Utes owned the Rockies. The Utes had been there forever. They would only be demeaning themselves to ask the white man for something they already owned. However, Ouray pressed the matter and Nevava finally gave in, allowing Ouray to go to the Pikes Peak region to see what the whites were up to. Ouray came back to report that tens of thousands of whites were swarming over the mountains and often shooting at the Utes on sight. He was already convinced that it was only a matter of time before the gold-and-land crazy white man would take over all the Ute territory.

Nevava still would not talk of signing a treaty; he felt that the Utes could stop the soldiers with sticks and stones if necessary as they came over Ute or Mosca passes. But Nevava was getting old and weak and it was time for a successor. Ouray called a tribal council and succeeded in convincing the councilmen to remove most of Nevava's powers and appoint Ouray himself to try to work out a treaty. Ouray immediately contacted his old friend Kit Carson, who started treaty negotiations, but warned that the white man only seemed to honor treaties as long as they felt they were favorable to them.

In 1860 and 1861, quite a bit of shuffling was done at the Ute agencies. The Tabeguache Utes were placed under the Denver agency and the Weeminuches were stationed at Tierra Amarilla in present day New Mexico. The Mouaches and most of the Jicarilla Apaches were moved from the Taos agency and attached to the Maxwell Ranch at Cimarron in present day Colorado. The Capotes continued to be handled at Abiquiu. In 1861, the Tabeguache Ute agency was again switched to Conejos, and Lafayette Head was appointed the first agent. In 1861, Kit Carson resigned as Indian agent to enlist in the Union Army, and he was replaced by Lafayette Head. One of the first things Head did was to hire Ouray as an interpreter and treaty negotiator at a salary of $500 per year. Ouray began bargaining but soon realized he was being asked to give up land, making it impossible to protect what the Utes already had.

At the other end of the Ute territory in northern Utah, by executive order dated October 3, 1861, the Uinta Valley was set apart as a reservation for the Uintah tribe, and the remainder of the Uintah's land was taken without a formal purchase.

Meanwhile, Ouray's son continued to grow and learn the Ute ways. By age five Paron not only could ride well, but could stalk and shoot game. Then one day in the spring of the year, Paron climbed on his father's powerful and spirited war horse, Thunder Cloud. Even some of the Ute braves couldn't ride Thunder Cloud. The horse immediately ran wild, but Paron clung desperately to the mare until the horse ran under the dead limb of a tree, which speared the boy and knocked him to the ground. The accident left a jagged, forked scar on the boy's right shoulder for life. His bravery also gave him a new name—Little Chief.

During this time Ouray's sister Susan was stolen by the Ute's main enemy, the Arapaho. But luckily for her, the whites saved her from torture and soon got her back to her tribe. About June of 1863, tragedy again struck Ouray. He had gone east onto the Plains with about thirty warriors and a dozen women to take part in a buffalo hunt near present day Fort Lupton north of Denver. Ouray was supposedly taking Paron on his first buffalo hunt away from Chipeta. After two weeks of successful hunting on the Plains, the group was ready to return to the mountains. But the night before they were to leave, a hundred Sioux warriors attacked the camp,

The Maxwell Ranch near Cimarron was the Mouache Ute agency after Taos, and it also served as the agency for a good number of Jicarilla Apaches. This building was on the agency grounds but was not the agency building proper. The earliest Ute agencies were in what was to become New Mexico because U.S. citizens were not yet traveling extensively in the Colorado area. Later, as Colorado became more populated, the agencies were moved farther and farther north until the Utes were totally out of New Mexico and only held a very small portion of Colorado. (Denver Public Library)

eventually stealing half the horses, killing three Utes and taking Paron, whom Ouray had tried to hide under the blankets in his tepee. Ouray tried to follow, but eventually realized that his group was outnumbered and his main camp needed protecting. The boy was later either captured by or traded to the Arapaho, who changed his name to Ute Friday. He was raised by the Arapaho, who hated the Utes. And the Utes in turn hated the Arapaho, calling them "dog eaters" or "yellow skins."

Ouray in 1872 recounted that:
> the Utes had a fight with the Sioux on the Platt. We killed one Indian, and knew it was a Sioux by his shirt, which was of a peculiar kind worn only by the Sioux. After the fight, my boy, about five years old, was missing; and a Mexican who traded with the Sioux has since told me that Friday (an Arapaho chief) had my boy, and a Mexican woman who was married to a Sioux also told me a year ago that she had seen my boy, and that Friday still had him.

For over a decade Ouray did not know the whereabouts of his son, but this event was to play an important part in the Brunot

Treaty of 1873. The loss was especially great because Chipeta was unable to have children. Ouray must have loved her very much because a Ute, especially a great chief, could have taken another wife. Ouray and Chipeta did, however, take in three children and reared them to adulthood. But Ouray never fully outlived the tragedy of the kidnapping of his only child. It was to haunt him the rest of his life.

In the 1870s, it was a common sight for the residents of Denver to see the Utes' tepees set up on the plains to the west, just outside the city limits. For six years, there was an agency at Denver, and the Utes, who often came out of their accustomed mountain terrain to hunt buffalo on the plains, soon became attracted to city life. A study of the tepee in the foreground illustrates how the smoke hole is held open by a supporting pole. The door is composed of a blanket, and the stakes holding the bottom of the tepee down can be clearly seen. This appears to be a hide covering rather than government-issued canvas. (Colorado Historical Society)

Chapter Four

THE TREATY OF 1863—
OURAY BECOMES A NEGOTIATOR

Ouray's reputation as a treaty negotiator began in earnest in 1862 when Ouray, other Utes, and the Conejos Indian agent Lafayette Head went to Denver. There they offered Territorial Governor John Evans the friendship of the Utes, provided that they be allowed to keep their traditional Colorado and Utah territory plus receive annual payments, rations and five Virginia stallions. Since the United States was not only in the midst of the Civil War, but was also faced with a possible Comanche uprising to the east, Evans readily agreed. The Utes received the Gunnison-Uncompahgre country "forever." However, this promise came only from the Territory of Colorado and not from the U.S. government. In February of 1863, a delegation of Utes which included Ouray was taken by Agent Head to Washington, D.C., New York and other large cities. The itinerary even included a meeting with President Lincoln, where they were promised many gifts. The main purpose of the trip, however, was to impress the Utes with the numbers and power of the white man, and thus make them more amenable to accepting a treaty giving up a sizable portion of their lands. It was reported that the Utes were told in Washington that the United States government would wipe them out if they made a disturbance.

Upon the homeward journey, the Utes passed through St. Joseph, Missouri, where the **Herald** of that city reported:

> These Utes are noble specimens of the Native Americans, with all the pride and obstinacy peculiar to the race. While in Washington they threw themselves upon their "reserved rights" refusing to make a treaty, and when an intimation was given to their spokesman that he had better conduct himself with propriety and not be so haughty he promptly told the Commissioner something like this: "I and my party came here because we wished to come. You may give presents to the other Indians, but we don't want any presents. You want our land because there is plenty of gold there, but all that you are willing to give us is copper. Do you think we are fools? You talk as if you could whip us. You are now fighting with your own brothers and can't whip them. You will find it harder

work to whip us. We wish to go home, and when we get there we may be willing to make a treaty."

On the way home, the Utes were escorted by hundreds of soldiers and civilians because it was necessary for them to pass through

This is a photograph of the residence, mill and general store belonging to Lafayette Head at Conejos, Colorado. Head became a political boss in the upper Rio Grande Valley and founded the town of Guadalupe just across the river from Conejos. He also ran the Ute Indian agency from here. Some said that the Indian goods had a way of ending up in his store instead of being distributed. Head also raised cattle, which he sold to the Indians. It was not at all uncommon for early day Indian agents to try to maneuver to get contracts so that they might make a hefty profit for themselves. (Colorado Historical Society)

Cheyenne, Arapaho and Comanche territory. Major Downing led the group. As they approached Julesburg on the South Platte River in the northeast corner of Colorado Territory, they were warned of an impending attack. Some Utes wanted to attack first, but instead —some say at Ouray's suggestion—the Utes were stripped of their weapons and the group proceeded. The hostile Indians surrounded Downing's band, which kept pushing on. Finally, reinforcements met the group and they continued on safely to Denver.

On October 1, 1863, Ouray was asked to serve as translator at a treaty conference called by the United States for the Tabeguache and Mouache Utes at the home and agency of Major Head at Conejos, Colorado. Representatives of all the Ute bands were

John Evans was the governor of Colorado in 1862 when he was visited by a delegation of Uncompahgre Utes accompanied by agent Lafayette Head. The Indians were seeking a promise that they would not be deprived of their recognized territory in the heart of Colorado. Since they were, for all practical matters, already confined to that portion of the domain lying west of the Continental Divide, the Utes also asked for annuity payments, provisions, and "five Virginia stallions," presumably to improve their strain of Indian ponies. Evans had such confidence in Ouray, who was not yet officially the overall chief, that he made the treaty anyway, presuming that Ouray would be able to convince the other Utes to go along with it. (Colorado Historical Society)

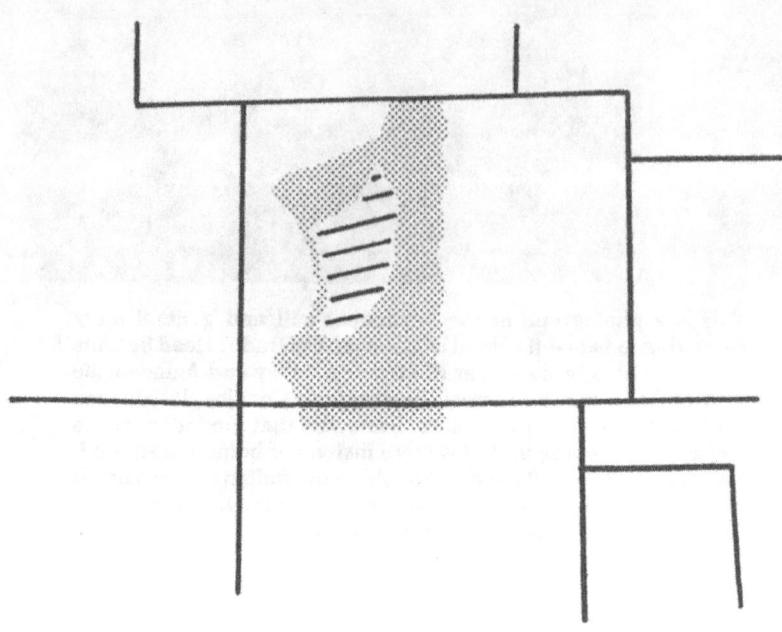

TABEGUACHE TREATY 1863

In 1863, a treaty was made in which Ouray was recognized by the United States as head of all the Utes, although at the time he could truthfully be called only a leader of some of the Tabeguache band. The treaty moved the Utes back from the eastern slope of the Rockies and the San Luis Valley. The shaded portion of this map shows the area which the Tabeguache and Mouache bands were recognized as controlling (although in fact they didn't). The Utes were to give up all but the area indicated by hatch marks. Since only the Tabeguache and a few Mouache Utes were at the treaty talks, the Treaty of 1863 wasn't recognized by most Utes and had to be affirmed by the other tribes in 1868.

supposed to have been present, but most of the Northern Utes were absent. Since many of the Ute bands were not there and some of the tribes did not wish to be part of the treaty, the United States government simply recognized the Tabeguache band as the "owners" of all the land it was after. The only real justification for this was that the Tabeguache were the largest group of Utes.

The United States was represented at the conference by Simeon Whitely, agent for the Grand River and Uintah Utes; Lafayette

From left to right in this photo are D.C. Oakes, Kit Carson, Lafayette Head and Hiram P. Bennett. In 1868, all four of these men traveled with the Utes to Washington, D.C., in pursuit of a treaty agreement. This picture was probably taken in Washington at that time. The Treaty of 1863, in which Lafayette Head and Kit Carson played a major part, had never really been enforced because only the Tabeguache band had been represented at the negotiations. In 1868, the United States tried once again to reach an agreement. Oakes had been appointed head agent of the White River Utes in May of 1865 and oversaw the building of the agency that later would be manned by Meeker. (Colorado Historical Society)

Head, agent for the Tabeguache Utes; Michael Steck, superintendent of the Southern Ute agency; John Evans, governor of the Territory of Colorado and Superintendent of Indian Affairs; and John Nicolay, secretary to President Abraham Lincoln, who also served as secretary of the treaty commission.

Ouray translated the talks from Ute to Spanish, and three Spanish interpreters translated from Spanish to English. From Conejos, a correspondent of the Denver **Commonwealth** wrote on

October 2, 1863:
> The Governor, Col. Chivington, Lieut. Col. Tappan, and other prominent officers of the Colorado troops

In the nineteenth century, it was common for an artist to make a sketch from a photograph so that it would reproduce better in books or magazines. This sketch was made from an earlier picture of Ouray and his brother Quenche. The photograph is thought to be the first picture ever taken of Ouray and the only one ever made of his brother. It appears in a French book, Le Tour Du Monde (The Tour of the World), published in 1868. The book mentions that Ouray (spelled Yule′) was one of the chiefs participating in the 1863 treaty conference. It is interesting to note Ouray's youthful look (he would have been thirty-one or thirty-two at the time) and Quenche's resemblance to Ouray. (Denver Public Library)

are here. It is the current belief of those who ought to know that the Utes will make no acceptable treaty, unless force be used to compel them to; and it is equally the general opinion that force will be used ... We are expecting six companies and a battery of artillery from Fort Union, which added to the troops already here, will make a force capable of whipping two Ute nations.

The Tabeguache refused to be moved to a new location, but they did agree to a treaty which defined the boundaries of a reservation for them and the Mouaches. On October 7, 1863, the treaty was signed by ten of the Utes, including "U-Ray or Arrow," who made his (x) mark. The federal government had generally recognized Ouray as head chief of the Utes because, during his presence at the meeting, he had shown considerable prestige and influence. However, at the time, Ouray was not considered a particularly powerful chief by the Utes. In fact, he was never at any time considered by all the Utes to be their overall chief, in part because the Utes didn't pick Ouray themselves and in part because Ouray's later actions were always controversial.

The treaty of 1863 gave up the San Luis Valley and those portions of the mountains which were already settled including most of the territory east of present day Gunnison, Colorado. The Utes admitted the supremacy of the United States, agreed that the United States could establish military posts on their land, and allowed the U.S. to establish roads, railroads and mail lines (including mail stations) within the reservation. It was specifically agreed that miners could come on the Ute land to seek and mine gold and other minerals or metals. The Mouache Utes were to be moved onto the same land as the Tabeguache. It was further agreed that if any Ute committed a crime, he would be turned over to the United States government for punishment, and that if a white committed a crime against a Ute, he "shall be tried, and if found guilty, shall be punished in like manner as if the injury had been done to a white man."

In return the Utes were to receive ten thousand dollars in goods and ten thousand dollars in provisions each year for a period of ten years. There was also provision for five stallions for breeding purposes, and up to 750 cattle and 3,500 sheep were to be given to the Utes if they were willing to take up farming or stock raising. The government was also to supply a blacksmith and blacksmith shop to repair the Ute guns and agricultural implements. Between ten thousand and fifteen thousand pounds of gifts were shipped to Conejos to be delivered to the Utes.

Eventually, the annuities became a problem. The United States House of Representatives sometimes forgot to appropriate the money because the country was totally immersed in the Civil War. In addition, it was hard to get the goods into the rough and rugged Ute territory. Furthermore, it was sometimes impossible to locate all the Utes in order to distribute the goods evenly, and when the Indians were found, it was hard to tell if they were Utes or some other tribe. However, the treaty was ratified by the U.S. Senate on March 25, 1864, and silver medals were awarded to the Ute signers.

From this experience, Ouray learned a lesson. He would have to give up some Ute land to get a guaranty of the Utes' rights to that land which was remaining. In order to convince the scattered Ute bands to accept the treaty he so brazenly had signed, Ouray tried to gain power by patience, threats, bribes or political diplomacy and maneuvering. He began to formulate the idea that the Utes should protect themselves, not by fighting, but by bargaining with the whites. He was evidently trying to find a middle course between the two cultures. Ouray also hoped that Utes would reduce their hunting grounds and start raising cattle and crops, and that they would trade buckskins and other items with the whites. However, his control over any of the Ute bands other than the Uncompahgres was precarious. Many of the other bands felt that he was selling the Utes out.

In 1864, heavy snows prevented the Utes from gathering their usual winter supplies of buffalo meat, and the Tabeguache Utes did considerable begging in Colorado Springs that winter. Friction began to arise in the San Luis Valley also. On November 29, 1864, on the plains of eastern Colorado, the infamous Sand Creek Massacre occurred. Colorado volunteers under Militia Colonel John M. Chivington (a Methodist minister also called "The Fighting Parson") attacked friendly Cheyenne Indians under the leadership of Black Kettle, killing men, women and children. Chivington discovered one of his men trying to hide a young Indian boy and reminded him that "nits become lice"—his words became famous among Indian fighters of the West.

Up until this time little attempt had been made to restrict the Utes to the reservation. However, in 1865 the United States began

This picture is supposed to be a very early day photograph of Chief Ouray and is often attributed to W.H. Jackson. If it is a Jackson, it could not have been taken any earlier than 1874 when Jackson first came to Colorado and Ouray was forty years old. In the picture, Ouray is wearing a peace medal that could have come from either the 1863, the 1868 or the 1873 treaty negotiations. The cane in his right hand may well have been a gift from President Lincoln in 1863. Lincoln often gave these canes to Indian chiefs to show his gratitude for their cooperation and friendship. Tradition has it that when Ouray and twelve other Utes met Lincoln, the President stepped forward and shook hands with Ouray first, thereby giving Ouray an edge on being named the first overall chief of the Utes. (Colorado Historical Society)

to decide that the Utes should be moved off of the Front Range. In May of 1865, a delegation of Utes went to see Governor Evans in Denver, and in July of that same year, Evans reciprocated and went to visit with the Utes. In 1865 at the Conejos Indian agency, Lafayette Head began grooming a young man named Otto Mears to take over his job as agent. Mears was to become extremely familiar with the Ute customs and was one of the few white men that was ever able to speak the Ute language fluently. Before long Mears had an official contract with the U.S. government allowing him to trade with the Utes. He quickly earned the Utes' respect and figured prominently in Ute affairs from this point on.

Then, in 1866, an attempt was made to negotiate another treaty which would force the Utes to settle down on the reservation. The council was held among cottonwoods near the site of present day Alamosa, Colorado. Kit Carson acted as interpreter, while Ouray was the chief spokesman for the Utes. Territorial Governor Cummings urged the Utes to accept a reservation, settle down, and live like the white people. The Indians were adamantly against this proposal because, if they stayed permanently in one place, they explained, their enemies could easily find and murder them. LeRoy R. Hafen, former Colorado State Historian, quotes Ouray as saying (although it is suspected that the reporter at the meeting added to what Ouray said):

> Long time ago, Utes always had plenty. On the prairie, antelope and buffalo, so many Ooray can't count. In the mountains, deer and bear, everywhere. In the streams, trout, duck, beaver, everything. Good Manitou gave all to red man; Utes happy all the year. White man came, and now Utes go hungry a heap. Game much go every year—hard to shoot now. Old man often weak for want of food. Squaw and papoose cry. Only strong brave live. White man grow a heap; Red man no grow—soon die all. Utes stop not in one place, and Comanches no find. But Utes settle down; then Comanches come and kill. Tell Great Father, Cheyennes and Comanches go on Reservation **first**; then Utes will. But Comanches first.

General Rusling, who attended the council, summarized the results:

> The Governor re-hashed his arguments, and presented them anew in various ways; but to all of them Ooray steadily made answer: "Ooray has spoken!" and there the matter ended.

The treaty council was a failure. General W.T. Sherman, who was one of those representing the whites, is reported to have said in disgust after the meeting: "They will have to freeze and starve a little more, I reckon, before they will listen to common sense."

That same year, a small group of Utes raided the settlers on

On November 29, 1864, John Chivington and his men attacked the Cheyenne and Arapahos who were under the leadership of White Antelope, Black Kettle and Left Hand. Nothing had been done to provoke the attack, which began while the Indians were sleeping. It is estimated that as many as three hundred Indian men, women and children were killed that day. Some whites defend the soldiers' actions by arguing that the Indians were attacked in retaliation for atrocities they had committed in the past. Others call the attack a massacre that far exceeded any provocation committed by the Indians. At any rate, the Sand Creek Massacre put fear into the hearts of all Indians, including the Utes, who felt that such an unwarranted slaughter might also happen to them someday. (Colorado Historical Society)

Huerfano Creek, and Ouray sent runners to warn other settlers. Ouray himself followed and helped take the hostile Utes prisoner, then delivered them to Fort Garland, where they were jailed.

In September of 1866, General Sherman visited Ft. Garland. Kit Carson was commander, and meetings were again held with the Utes. Sherman was impressed at the way Carson was able to deal with the Indians. He noted that Ouray was very influential among his people and that he was also on very good terms with Kit Carson.

As the Civil War came to an end, more trouble was in store for the Utes. Treaties were soon signed with the Arapahos, Cheyennes, Apaches, Comanches, and Kiowas. The Utes were the only Indians left to deal with in the Colorado Territory. The Reconstruction government, bogged down with bureaucracy, considered Indian agents' jobs as political favors to be given out. Most of the agents were not prepared for their work, and others were downright dishonest. If the United States government even remembered to

make its payments, the funds were often lost or the money misappropriated before it got to the Indians.

By 1867, the United States was already substantially in arrears on its payments. The government also failed to provide any of the much needed animals and goods which had been promised. The winter of 1866-67 was very harsh, and almost a thousand Utes under Shavano and Colorow again went begging for food in the Colorado Springs area. To compound the problem, the Utes hadn't changed their habits and continued to go wherever they wanted. Their lot in life was not good. Samuel Bowles wrote in 1868 of a band of Utes he met in Middle Park:

> They look frailer and feebler than you would expect; I did not see a single Indian who was six feet high or would weigh over one hundred and seventy-five pounds; they are all, indeed, under size, and no match in nervous or physical force for the average white man ... Their square heads, coarse hair, hideous daubs of yellow and red paint on the cheek and forehead, any motley raiment,—here a white man's cast-off hat, coat or pantaloons, if squaw a shabby old gown of calico or shirt of white cloth, alternate with Indian leggins and moccasins, bare legs and feet, a dirty white or flaming red blanket, beaded jacket of leather, feathers, and brass or tin trinkets hanging on the head, from the ears, down the back or breast,—all these disorderly and unaccustomed combinations give them at first a repulsive and finally a very absurd appearance.

In June of 1868, Chief Nevava died. The northern bands were in turmoil trying to decide who would be his successor. Antelope, Douglas, Johnson, Colorow and Captain Jack were all candidates. Ouray suggested that one solution to the problem would be that they all remain subchiefs since Ouray was now officially the head chief of all seven Ute bands. None of the subchiefs liked this idea, however, and eventually Douglas assumed an uneasy leadership position.

Chief Colorow (also called "Colorado") was one of several chiefs who continually fought for control of the Northern Utes. Colorow gorged himself so much during meals that he eventually weighed over three hundred pounds. He took pleasure in frightening women and children. Many of the whites of his time felt that Colorow was representative of all Indians, when in fact he was perhaps the most uncharacteristic of all the Ute men. (Colorado Historical Society)

Chapter Five

THE TREATY OF 1868— NEW AGENCIES

By 1868, it was obvious that another treaty would be necessary, in part because not all the Utes had joined in the previous one, and in part because territory that was assumed to be Tabeguache was not in fact theirs. Ouray had generally succeeded in taking control of the seven bands, and the United States government officially appointed him chief spokesman for the Utes in the negotiation of the treaty. Ouray suggested to then Governor Alexander Hunt that the Ute Indians again go to Washington since Ouray knew he couldn't enter into a treaty alone. The Northern Utes were upset that Colorow or one of their subchiefs was not picked as head spokesman and that Ouray had previously given up territory that they considered to be theirs, at least in part. Only Douglas, Captain Jack and Colorow openly backed Ouray. Many of the Southern Utes under Ignacio did not support Ouray at all.

So in January of 1868, Ouray, Mouache Chief Kaneache, White River subchiefs Captain Jack and Sowerwich, the late Chief Nevava's nephew Piah, and five other chiefs traveled with Kit Carson and D.C. Oakes to Washington to make the treaty. There was a lot of tough bargaining. During this time Ouray made his famous statement that "the agreement an Indian makes to a United States treaty is like the agreement a buffalo makes with his hunter when pierced with arrows. All he can do is lie down and give in."

The Treaty of 1868 (or Hunt Treaty) was signed by the chiefs on March 2, 1868, and set forth what were thought to be the first definite and exclusive boundaries of the Ute territory. The treaty recognized 15,120,000 acres (roughly the western third of Colorado) as Ute lands that they were to, again, keep "forever." No white man was to pass over, settle upon or reside on Ute land. The land set aside averaged almost five thousand acres per Ute; however, in the rough mountain terrain a large amount of land was necessary for the nomadic Indians. The Utah border was the western edge of the territory; the 107th meridian (two miles west of present day Gunnison) was the eastern border. Present day New Mexico was the southern border, and the northern boundary was the present northern edge of Rio Blanco County (about fifteen miles north of Meeker). The Indians were basically giving up their traditional territory in the San Luis Valley, the Yampa River Valley

Some of the Indian delegates, their representatives, and those of the United States government are shown here in Washington, D.C., on the occasion of the 1868 treaty negotiations. From left to right are Lafayette Head, Conejos Indian agent; Wara; Donald C. Oakes; a very young and powerful-looking Chief Ouray; Edward H. Kellogg (brother-in-law of Governor Hunt); Capote; and William G. Godfrey. The photograph was probably taken by Matthew Brady or one of his assistants; Brady seems to have pretty well sewed up the "official" Washington photographs of the time. (Colorado Historical Society)

and Middle and North parks, most of which the whites had already taken away.

The various Ute bands eventually ratified all of the provisions of the Treaty of 1868, although it was late September before all the Utes were contacted. By signing this treaty, the Indians also ratified the Treaty of 1863. The United States agreed to establish two agencies, one for the Grand River and Yampa bands on the White River, and one for the Tabeguache, Mouache, Weeminuche and Capote bands on the Rio de los Pinos. At each of the agencies, the United States was to build a warehouse, a schoolhouse and houses for the agent, a carpenter, a farmer, a blacksmith and a miller. A water-powered sawmill with gristmill and shingle machines was also to be built. Agents were to reside at the agency to hear complaints from the Indians.

In an effort to force the Indians into farming, homestead provisions were built into the treaty. The head of any family could claim 160 acres of farmland within the reservation as his personal property. He would also receive seeds, implements and instructions on farming. Any Ute over eighteen that wasn't the head of a family could get eighty acres. Carpenters, millers, farmers and blacksmiths were to be furnished as needed. A teacher was to be assigned to each agency, and Ute children between the ages of seven and eighteen were to attend school. The Utes were promised up to $30,000 per year for thirty years for clothing, blankets and other articles of utility. They were also awarded an additional $30,000 for food, and each head of a lodge was to receive "one gentle American cow, as distinguished from the ordinary Mexican

This photograph presents more of the delegates to the 1868 treaty negotiations. From left to right are George M. Chilcott, delegate from the Territory of Colorado; Sa-wa-ich; Colonel Albert Boone, grandson of Daniel Boone; Governor A.C. Hunt of the Colorado Territory; Captain Jack, who later played an important part in the Meeker Massacre; and Hiram C. Bennett, who was also one of the first delegates from Colorado to the United States Congress. Kit Carson was also with the group but for some reason was not photographed in this shot to honor the occasion of the Ute Indians' visit to the Capitol. (Colorado Historical Society)

or Texas breed, and five head of sheep."

The Utes were told repeatedly that the land deeded to them in the treaty would be theirs forever and that no whites would be allowed to trespass on it. The treaty specifically provided that the United States **solemnly** agreed that no person, other than certain government officers, would be permitted to pass over, settle or reside on the reservation. However, there was an important exception. "Roads, highways and railroads, authorized by law" were allowed through the reservations.

Ouray (by making his mark beside "U-re") and nine other chiefs signed the treaty March 2, 1868. Forty-seven chiefs of the other bands ratified the treaty later, including Ouray making his mark beside "Ou-ray." (It is also interesting to note Ouray signed as a Mouache not a Tabeguache.) Three-fourths of the adult male Utes had to approve this and all other Ute treaties before they could take effect. This was an important stipulation that was to slow down the ratification of all future treaties. An amendment was added August 15, 1868, by Ouray signing as "Ouray," which granted him a pension of $1,000 per year—a fact which made many of the other Utes furious.

The 1868 treaty contained all the elements of Ouray's strategy for the Utes. The Utes would cease to be nomads and begin to farm and ranch. At last, definite boundaries for their territory were reserved for them, and they were assured no white man would bother them. Honest Indian agents were to make certain the Utes got their rations and supplies. It was probably one of the best treaties ever negotiated by any Indian. But the peaceful relations that seemed assured did not materialize and problems arose almost immediately. Ouray's friend, Kit Carson, died on the way home. When the surveyors came with their chains, compasses and stakes to settle the reservation's boundaries, it was discovered that many of the high parks—the Utes' best hunting country—were now U.S. territory. The Utes weren't used to imaginary boundary lines. Their boundaries were the more recognizable ridges, rivers and valleys of Colorado. As if this weren't bad enough, the prospectors just kept right on coming into Ute territory. Ouray at first refused to sign the ratification of the survey and protested the trespasses, but to no avail. After the government promised to send soldiers to guard the reservation, Ouray signed, but when the whites objected to the troops, they were withdrawn.

Because their domain was restricted for the first time by treaty, the Utes could not spread out over the large territory that they had previously used for hunting. The Indian agents were issued orders to keep the Utes on the reservations. This meant (and the treaty provided for) a supply of rations and clothing by the U.S. government to supplement what food the Utes could obtain by hunting until they could be trained in agriculture. Because the Utes had to reduce their territory and take up stock raising, farming and trading, the government was able to keep a better eye on them.

Although the treaty was signed in 1868, it was not until April 10 of the following year that the U.S. Congress gave President Grant the power to resettle the Indians on whatever reservation land would be best to support them. The treaty called for two Indian agencies, but three were eventually built. One was on the White River near the present town of Meeker. It was meant to serve the approximately eight hundred Yampa and Grand River Utes. Its first agent was Charles Adams, who was also to play a part in the Alferd Packer episode mentioned later. A second (the unofficial) agency was started in Denver on January 17, 1871. Major James B. Thompson served as its first agent. Although Denver was outside the reservation, the Utes insisted on coming to that area to hunt buffalo, even though by that time the buffalo was almost extinct. The people of Denver welcomed the agency because of the money it brought to town.

The White River and Mouache bands came often to the area, generally pitching ten to twenty tepees at Red Rocks. They also camped in a large cave nearby which became known as "Colorow's Cave." Colorow was a chief who grew more and more fond of the white man's food. He regularly appeared at doors on the outskirts of Denver where housewives usually gave him bread or biscuits with mounds of sugar or sweet syrup. On this diet, Colorow's great frame began to fill, eventually reaching a weight of 300 pounds.

The Mouaches were entranced with play-acting and frequented the smaller theatres in the area. On occasion they put on some rather bizarre shows of their own. Each spring they performed the Bear Dance, to the delight of Denver's elite, but the final act (that put an end to the Denver Agency) was a Scalp Dance performed under the leadership of Piah. The fresh, bloody Cheyenne scalps were more than Denver's society could stomach. After six years of colorful existence, the Denver Ute agency was forced to close.

When it came time to actually place the Tabeguache, Mouache, Capotes and Weeminuches on the Los Pinos reservation, a strange twist occurred. Presumably the Utes didn't understand the boundaries of the treaty. The Uncompahgre Utes started towards the Los Pinos River (a tributary of the Los Animas in La Plata County), but they refused to go any further when they reached Cochetopa Creek about sixty miles north and fifty-five miles west of present day Saguache. The spot was not even within the boundaries of the reservation, but the Utes would go no further. To comply with the treaty, the U.S. government ended up renaming the creek! But even the government was confused. One of the local Indian agents wrote that "the reservation lies immediately in front of the Grand Canon of the Colorado ... not less than 150 miles from any traveled road, and over two great mountain ranges that usually become impassable by October 20 each year." Wrong on all counts!

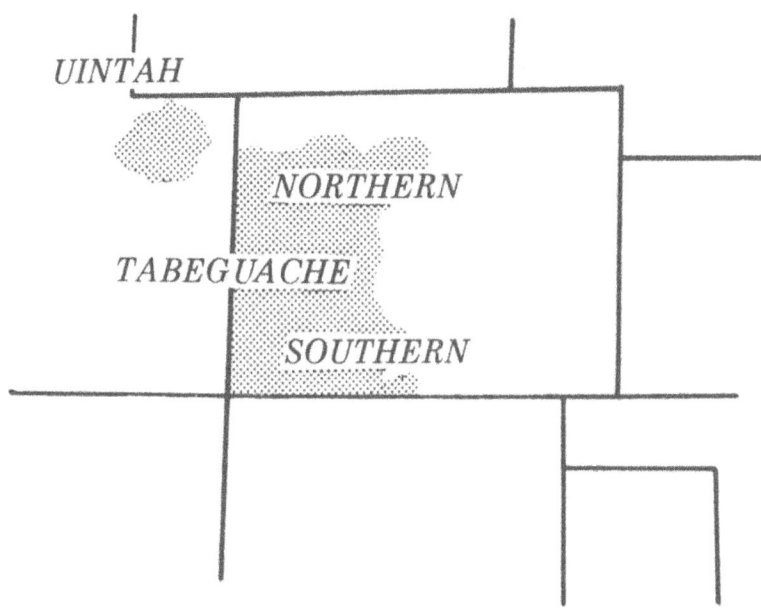

UTE TERRITORY 1868

By 1868, the Uintah Utes had been forced onto their reservation in what is now northeastern Utah. The Treaty of 1868 (or Hunt Treaty) set out the first clear and definite boundaries of Ute Territory. What is now the Utah border was the western edge, and the 107th meridian constituted the eastern. The New Mexico border of today was the southern boundary, and fifteen miles north of the 40th parallel was the northern edge. Generally, the Utes were receiving the western third of Colorado, which the whites solemnly agreed they could keep forever.

On June 12, 1869, General Edward McCook left Denver, accompanied by ten soldiers, to construct a sawmill at the site of the new Los Pinos agency, to be used to cut lumber for the new buildings. When he reached Saguache, he met his guide, Godfrey, who was to be in charge of the construction. Also at Los Pinos were a Mr. Matthews, who was an artist for **Harpers Weekly**, and R.B. Townshend, an Englishman traveling in America and who later wrote the book, **A Tenderfoot in Colorado**. Godfrey warned that Curtis, who was to be the interpreter with the Indians, had not yet

In 1875, Colorow and his band agreed to have their picture taken in front of Ben Gurnsey's photographic studio in Colorado Springs. Colorow's band was well armed and the second Indian from the left holds a new, or almost new, Maynard rifle. Colorow has his rifle in a fine buckskin case. He and his group would often threaten settlers, sometimes making motions as if they were going to scalp them. However, because Colorow was so outspoken in his opinion that the whites should not come into Indian territory, he did gain some local followers; and there is no doubt that the whites were scared to death of him because he was so unpredictable. (Colorado Historical Society)

arrived. He was afraid of the Indian reaction when the white men and soldiers began to move onto the reservation, but Matthews had heard of Ouray and wasn't worried. He told Townshend:

Oh, shucks! These Southern Utes ain't going to make trouble. It's nothing but chin-music to them. Ouray'll keep 'em quiet ... (he is) the big peace-chief of the whole Ute nation. He's not here; he's off somewheres else just now but he's an Indian with brains, and he's been to Washington and seen Uncle Sam's soldiers and rifles and cannons. He knows. When the Southern Utes kicked against the treaty he made three years back ceding to us the whole of the Wet Mountain Valley he told Chief Ignacio and the rest of 'em straight out, "my beloved brethren, it's no use your kicking; the white man has a gun for every tree." Oh, his head's level. He'll hold 'em down right enough, whatever old thing the Governor wants out of 'em.

Matthews had a different opinion about Shavano:

(He is) their head war-chief. Ouray's jest their head peace-chief; he may do the talkee-talkee business with the Government but Shavano's their real big man. He's a man-killer. He's killed more men than any other Ute, and they jest worship him, and he's got eight hundred warriors there.

But trouble did arise. When the three caught up with General McCook at his camp part way up Cochetopa Pass they found he had just received a worrisome message from Captain Alexander stating that the Uncompahgres had sworn they wouldn't follow the treaty. Ouray was temporarily absent and hadn't enough backing. Kaneache was the only chief who had nerve enough to back him, and because of this, the other Utes had thrown him out of camp. The militant Shavano was the chief in charge in Ouray's absence.

The next day they reached the Los Pinos agency. Townshend described the scene beautifully:

The new agency was in a lovely natural park on the Gunnison, and the first frosts had painted yellow and scarlet the quakenasp and dwarf oak that grew thick along the gulches. Every hill-top was crowned with the tall red-stemmed columns of pines, while the rich bunch-grass clothed all the slopes. The cone shaped tepees of the Utes stood in clusters, each band grouped, as its sub-chief chose, near wood and water. Naked Indian boys were driving wiry ponies back and forth through the grass, while other boys were coming up from the creek with strings of splendid trout and the gaily-dressed bucks rode in from the hills with dripping red lumps of fresh-killed venison and elk-meat hanging to their saddles. There were enough of them. The sawmill men swore they had counted five hundred tepees, and every frontiersman knows each tepee counts for at least two warriors.

The new agency was being built in the very middle of the park, and here the sawmill had been started, and the wagons set to hauling in logs to be sawn into timber to build with. This was the true sign of the white man's foot. Already mutilated tree-stumps stood where noble pines had been, yellow sawdust floated down the clear stream—the sawdust that kills the trout—and raw yellow skeleton buildings of unseasoned boards were being hammered together by clattering carpenters. No wonder the wild Uncompahgres felt the desecration and shouted for war. Yet even over the wild Indians who had never before seen a white man the General's word had power. He summoned the reluctant chiefs to council, and they came...

To and fro the tide of argument flowed. When the Uncompahgres grew too insolent, and threatened us openly, the General answered: "You may kill me and

During the time that the Ute agency was in Denver, many of the Utes found that life in the big city was rather fun. They enjoyed most of the white man's forms of entertainment, and they in turn would perform ceremonial dances to amuse the white population. The sporty white element took great pleasure in encouraging the Indians to dress up like the white man—in stove top hats and other formal attire—and then enjoyed watching them try to imitate the white man's airs. The Indians, having a quite normal human need for friendship, evidently believed that aping the white man would please him. (Colorado Historical Society)

General Edward M. McCook, brother-in-law of James B. Thompson, helped get the first Los Pinos agency established and in operation. McCook, among other things, set up the sawmill so that construction could start on the agency buildings. McCook was appointed Territorial governor in December of 1869, replacing Governor Hunt. One of his duties was to be the Superintendent of Indian Affairs, but he appointed Thompson to that post and also made him the Indian agent at Denver. Some speculate that the Denver agency was created to bring Indian money to Denver merchants. (Denver Public Library)

Lt. Calvin T. Speer was the first Indian agent at the Cochetopa site of the Los Pinos agency. He had great difficulty in getting the Indians to accept his presence on the agency grounds, for the treaty stated that no white man was to be on their land, and they believed that included the agent! Speer was the official agent from June 26 to July 23, 1869, but he ended up staying on for an extra year and a half because the wife of his replacement died before the man could assume his post, and his second replacement took his time getting his affairs in order and coming to Los Pinos. (Colorado Historical Society)

my ten men, but there are ten thousand more behind us, and ten times ten thousand behind them. Ouray has seen them. Ask him."

The General's confidence in Ouray carried weight; the Uncompahgres listened and at last they gave way. They accepted the treaty, and they received Kaneache back.

On July 31, 1869, the first agent, Lt. Calvin T. Speer, 11th U.S. Infantry, arrived at Los Pinos. Problems immediately arose. The

This picture of Otto Mears and Chief Ouray appears in many books and magazine articles and has been given almost as many dates. Mears began dealing with the Utes in Conejos in 1865 and was hired in 1869 to put a road into the Los Pinos agency from Saguache. D.C. Oakes was the interpreter at the 1868 treaty, but Otto Mears interpreted at the 1873 treaty. The clothes Ouray is wearing perfectly match those he has on in a picture taken August 19, 1874, in Washington, D.C., when Ouray and Mears returned to seek Ouray's "lost" son. The photo was probably shot by Brady or his associates because the floor covering is the same as that in photographs known to have been taken by him. (Denver Public Library)

Indians pointed out, very logically, that under the terms of their agreement, no white man was to live on the reservation—and to them this included the Indian agent! They told Speer to stay in Saguache. The Indians and Speer entered into negotiations for the next four days. Ouray began to voice his concern that the 1868 treaty was not being honored, while one of the chiefs whose name was signed to the treaty complained it had never been read to him. The cows, beef, and clothing that had been promised had not been received. Chief Unaneanance, backed by fifty warriors, declared that no white should settle on the reservation. But in the end, Speer's patience and promises won out and he began to do his job—setting up a working agency for the Utes. A mill which could produce four to five thousand board feet per day was established. By November 13, 1869, Speer was able to report to General McCook on the status of the new building program, which included houses for the agent, blacksmith and farmer.

There were soon fourteen white employees at the agency, a few with families. A schoolhouse large enough to house a missionary or teacher and to accommodate forty to fifty children was built, but unfortunately very few of the Indian children used it. Other improvements were soon to follow. A house for the carpenter was erected on the east side of the square between the house of the agent and the blacksmith. A house of hand-hewn logs, thirty-two feet by sixteen feet and containing four rooms, was built for Ouray to the southeast of the square. (This cabin later burned down with all the chief's belongings in it. The government reimbursed him $400 for the personal effects and a new cabin was built.) A hundred foot square corral with a twenty-five by one hundred foot stable was also constructed to house the horses, mules, cows and other livestock.

Otto Mears was hired to put in a road from Saguache to the agency so that supplies could be brought in. The road was a terrible mess, and on the average it took eleven days for the wagons to travel the sixty miles. Nor was Mears held in high esteem as a supplier of the cattle, potatoes and other goods for the agency. Speer reported to McCook in November, 1869, that Mears advised Russell not to brand fifty cows. He said he had old hides they could brand instead and account for the missing cattle by saying the cows died. Speer further noted that Mears was a Democrat, the party that "would stoop to any mean act to defeat the intentions of the government and he is assisted by every Democrat in Saguache."

In 1871, the agency's cow camp was established near present day Gunnison about thirty miles north of the agency. James P. Kelley was in charge at first and then Alonzo Hartman. One report counted 1,160 sheep and 640 cattle driven to the site by Charles F. Holt and John Kerr. The herd included five fine Durham bulls, but another report said that the rest of the cattle were "four hundred of the poorest, scrubbiest and ordinariest Texas cattle that ever passed through the territory." Two cowboys were always on hand to watch

This flour mill, which still stands near Saguache, Colorado, was constructed in 1873. It replaced a small, crude mill built by Otto Mears to allow local settlers an outlet for their harvests. The new mill was built by Enos Hotchkiss. Until they were moved to the Los Pinos II agency, the Tabeguache Utes, including Ouray and Chipeta, often came to the mill to have their grain ground into flour. Grain became a major cash crop for the whites in the Saguache area with the flour being sold in the new mining camps which were springing up throughout the region. (Colorado Historical Society)

the herds, but the cattle strayed all the way from the present day Gunnison area to Taylor Park, thirty miles to the north.

McCook's attitude toward the agency is expressed in a report to Indian Commissioner Parker, dated September 30, 1870:

> One-third of the territory of Colorado is turned over to the Utes who will not work and will not let others work. This great and rich country is set aside for the exclusive use of savages. A white man secures 160 acres by paying and preempting: but one aboriginal vagrant, by virtue of being head of a family, secures 12,800 acres without preemption or payment.

This photo, taken on the Gunnison County Courthouse steps in 1881, shows many of the early Gunnison pioneers. The second man from the left in the back row is Alonzo Hartman and to the extreme right of the picture is Sidney Jocknick. Hartman, was in charge of the Los Pinos cattle herd, which was kept near present day Gunnison. Sidney Jocknick spent at least one winter helping Hartman with the cattle. When the Indian agency was moved to the Uncompahgre location, Hartman stayed behind and became the first postmaster of Gunnison. Jocknick helped move the Indian cattle to their new location and stayed on for some time as an employee of that agency. (Denver Public Library)

Lt. Speer was officially relieved of his command on September 29, 1869, but he actually stayed until well into 1871 because his replacement, Jabez Nelson Trask, was delayed in coming to the agency due to the death of his wife. Trask finally arrived May 3,

1871, but lasted only through June of 1872. Trask was a Unitarian. By tradition various church groups recommended agents for the Indian agencies, and Los Pinos was allocated to the Unitarians. Trask was forty years old and a graduate of Harvard as well as Cambridge Divinity school. He was reported to be so anxious to get to Los Pinos that he didn't wait for transportation from Denver, but walked over 150 miles to the agency. He is described by Sidney Jocknick in his book, **Early Days on the Western Slope of Colorado**, as "an eccentric, of sterling honesty and guileless simplicity."

The Utes objected to Trask and by July 29, 1871, the state of affairs at the agency was such that J.F. Jocknick was sent from Washington to investigate. He had almost reached the agency on August 25 when about six miles from his destination, he was intercepted by a band of almost one hundred Tabeguache Utes. Ouray was present and also the subchiefs Sapovanero, Shavano, Chavis, Sawawatsewich, Jim, Bill and Ahanash. Ouray had heard in Denver of Jocknick's coming and had summoned the subchiefs to meet him in their camp.

The Utes made it clear they didn't like Trask. He shut himself up in the house, refused to issue rations, and treated them like dogs. He dressed in a peculiar manner, wearing green goggle eyeglasses and a high beaver hat. They wanted a man they could rely on for counsel and advice, mentioning especially Colonel Albert H. Pfeiffer, subagent, with whom they had formerly dealt in New Mexico. When Jocknick reached the agency, he reviewed the books and found them in total confusion—not through dishonesty, but rather through ineptness. It was also obvious that Trask had a complete lack of knowledge of the Utes.

Another reason for the Utes' dissatisfaction could have been found in Trask's conviction that gifts should not be given to the Indians to secure their cooperation. It also seemed that he was overly economical in expenditures. When his successor investigated assets, he found $25,000 banked in Denver upon which Trask might have drawn.

On Jocknick's return trip, he was met again by the Utes and remained with them overnight, spending the evening with Ouray and other chiefs. There was much dissatisfaction over the increasing encroachments of the whites and also concern at the uncertainty of boundaries. "No man knows within ten miles," asserted Jocknick, "the location of the 107th meridian," which was officially the Ute's eastern boundary. The feelings against Trask were so strong that Ouray volunteered to go to Washington at his own expense to ask for a change in agents. He pointed out that the President had promised him (when Ouray was in Washington in 1868) that he had but to ask and it would be granted.

Jocknick's estimate of Ouray is interesting:

> He is of little account as an interpreter for he has but limited use of English and Mexican. He speaks with remarkable facility. I think he has been much

overestimated. He is a remarkable Indian, but would not be much above mediocrity had his lot been cast among civilized Americans. Everybody lauds him as a sort of habit, but I do not think him above lending his influence to schemers, to seekers after the office of agent, or after opportunities to make money out of Agency business, and I know that the stuff he was represented as dictating to Governor McCook last summer was a mass of fabrication conceived for no good end. Still he is with all his self-conceit and self-will a man of good sense and of good advice among the Utahs, and is said to make a charitable use of the stipend he receives as interpreter.

After Jocknick's report, the Unitarian Church realized that the job was too much for the Harvard scholar and recommended his removal. As a result, John P. Clum replaced Trask on June 7, 1872. Bitterly, Trask said:

I did my work faithfully and efficiently, reduced expenses, had the confidence of the Indians, paid for Speer's cheats in invoice; and I shall see what is the honor of working in peril of health and life, working successfully, too, without a shadow of protection from my Government.

In the summer of 1872, General Charles Adams became the Los Pinos agent at a salary of $1,500 a year. This was supplemented by a stipend of $1,000 a year which his wife received as the agency teacher even though the schoolhouse was not used. Adams' actual name was Karl Adam Schwanbeck. He was a German by birth, but since his real name was so difficult to pronounce, he took the simple English name of Adams. The title "General" was a Colorado state militia title and a mark of respect.

Charles Adams was a good choice for agent at the Ute agency. He played an important role in negotiations and dealings with the Utes for many years to come, representing both the whites and the Indians very well. He was General McCook's brother-in-law, and Ouray trusted him.

Adams could tolerate the idiosyncrasies of the Utes. During the summer months, the Tabeguache Utes came to the agency in great numbers every ration day. As soon as flour, rice and other rations had been given out, the male Indians would take their rifles and revolvers, mount their horses and gather about the corral. As soon as they were assembled, they would whoop and yell until the cows stampeded, then they would follow in hot pursuit, shooting as if the frightened beasts were wild buffalo on the plains.

But trouble broke out almost immediately. In 1871, extensive gold and silver discoveries had been made in the San Juans within the Ute territory, and by 1872, whites were flooding into the area. A commission was appointed by the United States that year to negotiate for the San Juans, but Ouray at first refused to negotiate

"Issue day" at a Ute agency brought a large crowd, which would often camp on the agency grounds. Not only did the Indians come to get needed food, clothing, blankets and ammunition, but also to have a fine time socializing. The braves might ride in on their ponies, followed by their dogs and squaws. Beef was issued live and on the hoof so that the braves could run them down with their ponies, kill them in the manner of hunting buffalo, and then have the squaws skin and dress out the meat. This also solved for the government the problem of keeping the meat fresh in the days before refrigeration. (Denver Public Library)

another treaty since he was having trouble maintaining his position as head chief of all the tribes, especially with the Northern Utes. General Edward McCook became the territorial governor of Colorado at this time and began to misuse his powers as Superintendent of Indian Affairs. McCook wanted the Utes out of Colorado. Ouray constantly protested the flood of whites trespassing on Ute land, but to no avail. Ouray was caught in a situation where he could lead his braves into a hopeless war or negotiate again with the whites, who had already shown how long their word could be trusted. Neither result was good.

Finally, Ouray decided to negotiate in order to save as much of the Ute territory as he could. His biggest problem was to prevent Ute "hot bloods" from causing an incident that would give the United States an excuse to forget the treaties altogether and push the Utes completely out of their territory. When it became obvious that Ouray had decided to cede the San Juans, other Utes began to plot against his life. Ouray struck back relentlessly when he heard of this "treason." He didn't hesitate to kill and had an uncanny ability to shoot well under stress. Within four weeks he had killed five braves—Suckett, Dynamite, Jack of Clubs, Old Nick and Hot

Stuff, — adding threats and fear to his arsenal of persuasive tactics. Many of the Utes began to believe that Ouray was in a conspiracy with the United States government to sell out their land and to misuse their annuities.

In 1872, at the Los Pinos agency, Sapovanero (Chipeta's brother and Ouray's second-in-command) and four other subchiefs attempted to assassinate Ouray. They hid in the blacksmith's shop at the agency as Ouray came to get his horse shod. But George Hartman, the blacksmith, gave Ouray a warning wink, and when Sapovanero came charging out of the blacksmith shop with an axe, Ouray jumped behind a post and the blade passed by harmlessly. Sapovanero swung again but broke the handle of the axe. At this point, Ouray threw him into an irrigation ditch that ran past the blacksmith shop. Clutching his brother-in-law's throat, Ouray reached for his knife, but Chipeta, who happened to be nearby, yanked the knife away just as Ouray grasped at it. Sapovanero's accomplices fled. After that, in spite of the fight, Sapovanero was very loyal to Ouray, and, oddly enough, Ouray regained his trust in him. Whenever Ouray was away from the agency for any length of time, he usually left Sapovanero in charge.

Chapter Six

THE BRUNOT TREATY OF 1873— OURAY FINDS HIS SON?

Once Ouray realized the futility of trying to fight the whites, he agreed to further negotiations with the U.S. government. He had expected the United States to honor the 1868 treaty and couldn't understand why the Great White Father, who was supposed to be so strong and so powerful, couldn't control his people. The Utes had been promised that they could keep their land "as long as grass grows and water runs." Ouray had felt that with a mountain wall between the Indians and the whites, there would be peace, and trouble would come only if the whites poured over the range.

But the gold and silver seekers couldn't be stopped. The miners had been dealing with the Utes since the first gold strikes at Cherry and Clear creeks. They saw no reason why the Indians needed the gold and the silver. The Utes could move elsewhere, and the whites could gain quick and easy wealth.

A popular opinion of the day was published in **The Boulder News**:

> The Los Pinos Indian council has failed in its object. The Utes would not resign their reservation, so the fairest portion of Colorado and some of the richest mining country is closed by force of arms. So settled we believe it will be and should be. An Indian has no more right to stand in the way of civilization and progress than a wolf or bear.

Governor McCook, in his biennial message to the Colorado legislature on January 3, 1872, protested the size of the Ute reservation and stated that five or six thousand Indians (undoubtedly an overestimation) were occupying nearly thirty thousand square miles of land. He asked that a new treaty be secured, reducing the Ute territory or removing the Indians to another area altogether. The Colorado legislature responded quickly, requesting President U.S. Grant to obtain either a treaty reducing the size of the territory or Ute permission for miners to come onto their land. Grant, in the meanwhile, had decided to negotiate rather than wage war with the Indians. He created the United States Board of Indian Commissioners, which was a nonpartisan board of distinguished reformers who were to deal with the Indian issues.

In February of 1872, a warning was issued by the United States government for the whites to be out of the territory by June 1 or face being arrested. Troops were sent to push the men out if necessary,

This photograph of Piah, Chipeta's brother, is one of the few pictures obtained by William H. Jackson on the second day of his visit to the Los Pinos agency on Cochetopa Pass. Jackson was the official photographer for the Hayden Survey and purposely worked his schedule so that he would arrive at the agency on "issue day" in order to get good photos of the Utes. Jackson was to become one of the best-known photographers in the West, in large part because of his photographs of the Indians, Mesa Verde, the San Juans and Yellowstone. Jackson's photos were always an important part of Hayden's reports and are credited for the passing of the legislation that made Yellowstone a national park. (Colorado Historical Society)

but President Grant recalled them for the moment when he supposedly learned Ouray might be persuaded to cede the property after all. In April of 1872, three commissioners were appointed to negotiate with the Utes—Governor McCook, John D. Lang (a member of the U.S. Board of Indian Commissioners), and General John McDonald. Indian agent General Charles Adams brought Ouray, ten other Utes, and Otto Mears as interpreter to Denver in early July of 1872 to meet preliminarily with Governor McCook and

Prospectors poured into the San Juans with the discovery of gold and silver. This is a photograph of Howardsville in Baker's Park near present day Silverton. Charles Baker traveled into this park in 1860 and reported that the Utes were friendly but warned the miners not to settle on the land. As a result, the whites built few permanent structures, but they began demanding that the federal government do something to get the Utes out of the area. Howardsville was started before the Utes were actually gone, and by the summer of 1874 the settlement had progressed to the point shown in the picture. (Colorado Historical Society)

special agent J.B. Thompson. There it was decided that the Utes would hold the formal meeting with the appointed commissioners at Los Pinos in August. The president of the U.S. Board of Indian Commissioners, Felix R. Brunot, was also sent from Pennsylvania in early August of 1872 to join the three treaty commissioners in negotiating for the San Juan mining region. Basically, the United States was after a rectangular strip of the San Juan mountains that contained about four million acres and was about sixty-five miles wide and ninety miles long. Brunot was to try to explain that the prospectors could not be held back, that they would kill the Utes if necessary to get the gold and silver.

In fact, the white man had already entered the land in question over a decade before. In 1860, Captain Charles Baker and other prospectors had entered Baker's Park near present day Silverton in search of gold and silver. The group was carefully watched by the Utes. Although initially the prospects looked good, by August 8, 1861, the **Canon City Times** reported that the San Juan mining regions were abandoned even though all persons who had prospected there testified that every indication was favorable to a good yield of gold. It was reported that many prospectors had been killed by Indians and that some had perished from hunger and cold. In 1869, Sheldon Shafer and Joe Fearheiler entered the San Juan country from New Mexico. They ascended the Dolores River and in July found a promising discovery at the site of present day Rico, where they worked on the Pioneer Lode throughout the winter.

In 1869, a party of prospectors led by Adnah French (one of the members of the Baker expedition of 1860) headed for southwestern Colorado from Arizona. They prospected on the Mancos and Dolores rivers, and late in the fall reached the Animas River near old Animas City. Forced out by snow, the party wintered in New Mexico. In 1869 and 1870, Indian agent William Arny noted that there were many prospectors in the San Juan area and reported that he was constantly sending letters to the miners warning them that the Utes objected to their settlements.

Some prospectors sought permission from the federal government to work mines on the Ute reservation. They talked McCook into communicating with the Commissioner of Indian Affairs, who answered as early as 1870 that the Treaty of 1868 forbade any such activity. Despite this response, the Adnah French party set out in April of 1870 for the San Juan country and Baker's Park. They finally found true placer and lode claims. In his report as Superintendent of Indian Affairs in Colorado, Governor McCook wrote on October 13, 1870, that the Ute reservation included the most productive farming land in the territory as well as mines that would pay a man "$100 per day." On August 27, 1871, the first discoveries were made at the Ute-Ulay Mine near present day Lake City. By 1871, there were reports of ore coming from the area assaying as high as three hundred ounces of silver per ton.

The cartographers of the Hayden Survey were hard at work when William H. Jackson took this picture. The Hayden Survey, a forerunner of the U.S. Geological Survey, began its first efforts in Colorado in 1869 but worked in Wyoming and Montana between 1870 and 1872. The survey party returned to Colorado in 1873 and mapped the mountainous Ute area through 1875. In 1873, Lt. E.H. Ruffner, who was with the U.S. Army Corps of Engineers, surveyed the eastern Ute boundary under the Treaty of 1868 and on occasion ventured even farther into Ute territory. Since Wheeler, with the War Department, was also surveying in the area, the Utes certainly saw a lot of transits during that time. (Colorado Historical Society)

Ouray began to feel the pressure from the miners. In August, he traveled to the area with about twenty of his braves. He complained to Indian agent J.N. Trask that the prospectors were trespassing on Ute land. The agent went into the area and warned the prospectors to leave. An exchange of letters between Trask and Adnah French appeared in the June 20, 1872, edition of **The Pueblo Chieftain**:

Fort Garland, C.T. Dec. 9, 1871

Mr. Adnah French, Miner
Upper Animas, Ute Reservation
Colorado Territory

Last August I received complaint from chiefs of Ute Indians, that miners were trespassing upon their reservations. I made a journey as far as the upper Rio Grande and saw a few men to whom I stated the complaint and terms of the treaty, warning them to abandon all work and exploration upon the reservation. Afterwards I received special instructions from Department of the Interior to warn all miners and prospectors to quit the reservation forthwith. I have recently learned your name, and give by this letter the required warning, that you quit all work and exploration upon the reservation of the Ute Indians, and that you leave the reservation without delay, on peril of being prosecuted according to law ...

Respectfully,
J.N. Trask
U.S. Indian Agent

Mr. French responded:

Santa Fe, New Mexico
February 25, 1872

J.N. Trask
U.S. Indian Agent:

Your communication of Dec. 9, 1871, was received one week since ...

For your information I will state that the most friendly relations exist between the miners and the Indians. As I have stated before, we have been three years, on and off, prospecting and exploring that country, and much of the time have traveled and camped with the Indians, turning our stock into their herds, hunting, fishing and trapping with them, and from my earliest acquaintance with the Utes up to the present time I have not met with one who did not cordially and cheerfully extend the hand of friendship.

Last summer, in August, the great chief of the Ute Nation, old Ute (Ouray) with about 20 of his people, visited our mining camp on the Rio Las Animas. He seemed to be well pleased, and to use his own language, he said the Americans are a good people; go ahead and get all the gold and silver you want; and before he left he brought us a lot of fresh meat, and through many other sources I know to a positive certainty that the Old Ute does not wish to drive us out ... When we are made to understand and know, from some reliable source, that it is the wish of the government for us to abandon our project in that country, though hard and unfair it would seem, we will do so readily, or if we knew it was the unanimous wish of the Indians for us to leave, we would do so; but without this knowledge it would require a great many broken down preachers and carpetbaggers to dispossess us of our property ...

        Indignantly,
        Adnah French

This official-looking photograph was taken during the treaty negotiations of 1872, which were unsuccessful from the point of view of the whites, who were trying to get the Utes to move out of the San Juan Mountains. It looks like just about everyone connected in any way with the agency or with the negotiations was included in the picture. Only a few people in the photograph have been identified, but Territorial Governor Edward McCook is third from the left in the front row, and Colorow sits to the left of him. The black man in the back row has been identified as George Beckwith and the man to his right as Ouray. However, the second man from the right in the front row has also been identified as Ouray, but neither of the two really looks much like him. Note that virtually every Indian depicted has a white man's hat. (Colorado Historical Society)

Only Piah, with the long feather headdress, can be identified in this photograph, but he had talked several of his friends into posing with him on the second day of Jackson's visit to Los Pinos. In the afternoon of the first day, a thunderstorm developed. The medicine man was able to convince the more superstitious Utes that the "magic box" had produced the storm and that it was a warning that everyone would die if the camera continued to be used. Nevertheless, the next day Jackson was able to convince a few of the Indians to pose, but once again a thunderstorm interrupted the shooting. Three of the Utes wear peace medals (and hold Winchester rifles), and the center Ute displays a feather—for some reason a very common practice in early Indian pictures. (Colorado Historical Society)

By the summer of 1872, the substantial gold and silver strikes in the San Juans were known all over Colorado. Most of the Colorado Territory newspapers were printing reports of prospectors pouring into the area, and hand-picked ore, valued at over $30,000 per ton was coming out of the region. A fifteen-stamp mill was sent in. Although large numbers of miners started to spread out from the Baker's Park area into the territory around Lake City and Engineer Mountain, almost all the newspaper reports carried accounts that the Utes were friendly if they were even seen at all.

By 1872, ninety-five to a hundred miners had discovered claims in the San Juans. The Utes were, in fact, continuously demanding that the government make good the provisions of the treaty and keep the miners back. But the prospectors continued to return. On two different occasions, General MacKenzie and government troops were sent in to force out the trespassing prospectors, but to no avail. Each time, pressure was put on the government to obtain a new treaty, the troops were recalled, and another treaty attempt was made. But the Utes held to their rights.

August 18, 1872, was set as the date for a great meeting of whites and Utes at the Los Pinos agency. W.F.M. Arny, who was in charge of the New Mexico Indians, left Santa Fe on July 19 and arrived at the meeting site with eighty lodges of the Mouaches and twenty-four of the Capotes. The Weeminuches could not be persuaded to attend. The Tabeguache Utes were well represented by Ouray and Charles Adams. There was a delegation from Denver including James B. Thompson, the agent, as well as a delegation from White River and a small Jicarilla Apache delegation. Felix Brunot joined the meeting at the last momemt on August 24, 1872. The total number of Indians present, according to McCook and others, was approximately fifteen hundred or almost half of all the existing Utes.

The chiefs were presented by Ouray, after which an exhibition of the Ute War Dance ceremony was given. It was decided that a preliminary council would take place the following Wednesday, August 28. U.M. Curtis was chosen Ute interpreter of the Spanish language for the commission. The council was held in the schoolhouse, which was then being used as an officers' mess and storehouse. In the four-day council between August 28 and 31, the commissioners urged the Utes to sell the southern portion of their land. But they also assured them that the land was theirs, and that, in conformity with the Treaty of 1868, no force would be exerted to make them sell, or to remove them from any portion of, their reservation. Territorial Governor Edward McCook was the first to address the Utes. He explained that by Act of Congress on April 23, 1872, the whites were authorized to negotiate with the Utes for the southwest portion of their territory. "This must all be voluntary," he advised. "It is your land and we will give you a fair price." Then Lang spoke: "The Reds have been abused, wronged, cheated by bad white men, but there are white men who will treat you fairly.

Are you willing they should come in?" When Felix R. Brunot talked, he said, "White man has a farm he can't fence. He sells part of it, and takes care of the rest." He went on to explain that the Utes had much more land than they could use.

The Utes didn't react well. They knew that if they gave up some of their land, the miners would just move in and immediately push for more. As reported by the board of Indian Commissioners, Ouray expressed what was in substance also stated by the other Indian leaders:

> We do not want to sell a foot of our land—that is the opinion of all. The Government is obliged by its treaty to take care of our people, and that is all we want. For some time we have seen the whites coming in on our lands; we have not done anything ourselves, but have waited for the Government to fulfill its treaty. We have come here so that you may see that we are not satisfied with this trespassing on our lands; but we do not want to sell any of them.

On August 29, the second day of the conference, the Utes objected to the white man's words being written down, but it was finally agreed that the words of both parties should be written. Sapovanero, a Tabeguache chief, reiterated that the Utes did not wish to sell and the white man should be kept off. Kaneache, a Mouache chief, mistrusted the commission altogether. How did they know it was sent out by the President? He said he had heard that Governor McCook was working to get hold of the Ute lands and that Governor Arny was always working against the Utes.

McCook explained that the government wanted to extinguish the Indians' title and pay them money for their land. If not, the government would have to send soldiers to drive the miners out. On the third day, the Utes emphasized the fact that it was the government's duty to keep trespassers off their land. The Indians said they had no intention of assuming that obligation by using force to expel the miners. Ouray said he had given orders for his people to stay away from the mines and miners, and refused to interpret anymore, saying, "I will tell no more lies to my people." He said

Although this photograph is identified by many as being a Jackson picture, the props suggest otherwise; both the chair and floor coverings appear in photographs of General Grant, Kit Carson and General Custer, made by Matthew Brady in his Washington, D.C., studio. This is one of the few pictures of Ouray in which he is dressed mainly in white man's clothes (note his boots, shirt and vest). Ouray was also trying to grow a beard, which was very unusual for a Ute. However, the few scraggly hairs that eventually grew on his chin evidently looked so bad that he gave the idea up. (Colorado Historical Society)

the talk was making the Utes' "heart bad." The Utes left in an irritated state, but through the help of Ouray, they at least made the promise not to molest the intruding miners until spring.

The final report of the official commission merely said that undue

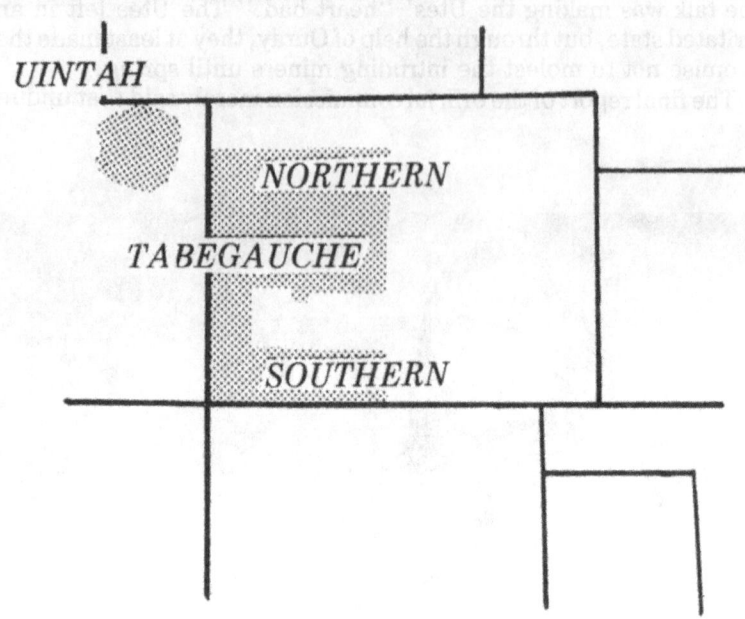

UTE TERRITORY 1873

In 1873, the Brunot Treaty carved the San Juan Mountains out of that territory which had been promised to the Utes forever. The treaty gave the whites the mountains but not the valleys, which they needed in order to supply grain, meat and vegetables to the miners. The slight notch in the otherwise rectangular ceded portion was made to allow the Utes to keep Uncompahgre Park, two miles south of present day Ridgway, which contained hot springs. To the Indians these springs were not only sacred, but they were therapeutic as well, helping to cure arthritis, rheumatism, and respiratory ailments.

influence on the Utes before the conference accounted for the failure to secure their objective, but they considered the conference beneficial. On Sunday, September 1, 1872, the commission left the agency.

Another delegation headed by General Edward Hatch was soon sent to Ouray. This delegation offered the Utes three alternatives: 1) they could voluntarily move to Indian Territory, now Oklahoma; 2) they could sell the entire southern portion of their reservation and concentrate in the north; or 3) they could give up the areas of the reservation now illegally occupied by the whites.

Ouray and the other chiefs of the tribe would not even talk about the first two proposals. They concentrated on the third. Ouray asked General Hatch: "Is not the United States government strong enough to keep its treaties with us?" Ouray pointed out that there had also been numerous violations of the previous treaties other than the prospectors coming on their land. Money had not been paid. Rations had not been delivered. Those rations that were delivered were often of very poor quality or even diluted or stolen by the whites. Much of the livestock that was promised was not delivered, and that which was delivered was of poor quality. Even though the government was supposed to be helping the Utes become ranchers and sheepherders, such things as the delivery of castrated rams and sterile stallions had taken place. On one occasion, twelve ewes and 1,908 castrated rams had been received.

Ouray pointed out that under the Treaty of 1868, the United States had basically received all that it had asked for. Now only four years later, after promising that the land would be the Utes' forever, the United States was asking for more. Ouray analyzed, dissected and shattered every proposition advanced by the government commissioners. He listened calmly and with dignified attention to everything they had to say, and then with eloquence and power, demolished every detail of their carefully arranged proposals. This government commission also returned to Washington in defeat.

The white man couldn't figure out what to do. The Utes were friendly Indians. If they had been hostile, their land would have been taken by force, but the Utes had even been allies with the United States in its wars against hostile Indian tribes. The United States government decided to try once again in late 1872. This time it wished to impress the Utes with the size and power of the United States, so Charles Adams was requested by the Commissioner of Indian Affairs to bring a delegation of Utes, selected by Chief Ouray, to Washington, D.C. for a conference with the Indian department and a meeting with President U.S. Grant. Ouray and Chipeta chose eight others to go with them, including Ouray's sister Susan, Sapovanero, and John McCook who was one of Chipeta's brothers. Ouray also asked Otto Mears to accompany them as an interpreter because Mears had learned the Ute ways and language well while supplying them with goods. Adams asked three other white men to go along and help Mears in looking after the delegation. The group left the agency on November 10, 1872, and traveled in a covered wagon to near present day Colorado Springs. There, they boarded a train for Washington, D.C.

The delegation spent ten days in Washington and met President and Mrs. U.S. Grant and their daughter in the White House. The Utes visited other big cities of the east and were taken to a circus, where they were fascinated by the trick riding and other per-

The caption beneath this picture reads, "Illustrated interview of our lady artist with the Ute Indian chiefs and prisoners in Washington, D.C.—from a sketch by Miss Georgia A. Davis." Whatever is meant by "prisoners" is not apparent. The man seated and reading the paper is evidently Chief Ouray, and the woman at the far left is undoubtedly Chipeta, who usually accompanied Ouray on his trips to Washington. The Indians were always a curiosity there, but the woman wearing the bustle must have looked just as strange to them—they must have wondered why the white women were so peculiarly constructed! (Denver Public Library)

formances in the arena. They were also taken to the zoo at Central Park, where they were especially impressed by the camels, the elephants (which they called "the big high animal with a tail at each end"), and the monkeys and baboons, which startled them at first, but which they later referred to as "the long armed creatures who try to look like men." The Utes finally arrived home at the Los Pinos agency on January 10, 1873, after a sixty-day trip with virtually nothing accomplished.

When it became obvious that the treaty efforts of 1872 had failed, the United States finally began to take steps to honor the Treaty of 1868. By February of 1873, general orders were issued to keep the prospectors out of the Indian's territory. Major A.J. Alexander, the commander at Fort Garland, sent copies of the orders to the Pueblo newspapers, which printed them in March of 1873. All prospectors were notified to leave the area by June 1 of that year or be removed

This Jackson photo depicts one of the camps of the Hayden Survey party of 1874, showing the pack animals laden with supplies but the tents in place. Beginning in 1867, the U.S. government established four major survey parties. Two of these operated through the War Department and two through the Department of the Interior, to which the Hayden party was assigned. Mr. Jackson accompanied the Hayden party on nine consecutive annual summer trips. During the winters in between, he would usually retire to Washington to make prints from the hundreds of negatives exposed the previous summer, which then needed to be identified, classified and filed. (Colorado Historical Society)

by military force, and to back up the threat, Alexander proceeded to move troops to the north of Del Norte (gateway to the San Juans over Stony Pass). The miners and the newspapers immediately protested. **The Denver Tribune** wrote on March 26:

> Now, however, that valuable mines have been discovered and opened up in San Juan with the prospect that a certain portion of the disputed district can be made available for agricultural as well as mining purposes, and hardy bands of pioneers have gone there with the avowed intention of staying and developing its resources—barbarism steps in, supported by the U.S. bayonets and says to civilization—"Stand back." Did there ever before exist such an anomalous condition of affairs; government interposing in behalf of a few straight-haired vagabonds against the property rights of a brave, energetic, intelligent class of white men?...

> That seven hundred American pioneers should be prodded out of the country by American bayonets, in order that a small band of dirty nomads can idly roam over 20,000,000 acres of hunting ground is an atrocity no other Government on the face of the earth but our own would be guilty of committing.

A mass meeting was held in Del Norte on April 23, 1873, to protest the action. Resolutions were passed, press releases sent out, the Southwestern and San Juan Miners' Cooperative and Protective Association was formed, and the following letter sent to the Secretary of the Interior by the group (a copy of which appeared in **The Denver Tribune**):

> For three years, we have occupied this country, unmolested; we have developed a greater wealth of mineral than has ever been seen upon this continent in so small a compass. Most of us have all our worldly possessions now invested in this country and to force us from it would be doing us an injustice and a wrong.
>
> We firmly believe that a treaty could be made with these Indians, by which they will be willing to relinquish their claim upon the southern portion of this reservation, from 38° 30' north to the southern boundary of Colorado....
>
>   D. REESE, President
>   J. CAREY FRENCH, Secretary

The government decided to back off again. The expulsion orders were revoked and steps were taken for another treaty council with the Utes. The miners were exuberant and thousands of new claims were staked that summer.

In the spring of 1873, Captain John Moss led a company of California miners into southwestern Colorado. They stopped at the mouth of La Plata Canyon and found both free placer gold and gold-bearing quartz. Captain Moss found Chief Ignacio of the Southern Utes and in a private treaty gained permission to mine and farm thirty-six square miles of the area. The Utes received one hundred ponies and a quantity of blankets in return.

That summer, the government also undertook to survey the Ute territory which had been established under the 1868 treaty. E.H. Ruffner of the Corps of Engineers was in charge of the survey, which he described in his account, the **Report of a Reconnaissance in the Ute Country Made in the Year 1873** (Washington, 1874). The party left Pueblo on May 7, 1873, traveled to the head of the Rio Grande River, crossed the Continental Divide, and descended Cunningham Gulch to Howardsville. They examined the various mining districts and investigated routes and trails. No general statement of the value or resources of the region was given in the report, although a good map was prepared and published. Ruffner

This shot shows a large part of the encampment of the Utes at the Los Pinos agency. Hundreds of Indians were in the area since it was "issue day," when supplies were given out. This was necessary because the Utes could no longer hunt buffalo on the plains of eastern Colorado. This photo was probably taken on the third day of Jackson's visit, for none of the Indians would now pose, and Jackson was forced to set up his camera in the door of the agency and take photographs from a distance. The Indians soon caught on and started throwing blankets in front of the camera, standing close enough to the lens to block the view and plucking the focusing cloth from Jackson's head, all the while threatening him with harm if he didn't stop. (Colorado Historical Society)

described the Utes he saw as: ..."mostly well-armed, well-mounted, well-dressed; uncommonly clean, smiling and civil. They were short men with broad muscular shoulders; good working for Indians; bland, courteous, and great beggars."

The government used another ploy to get the Utes out of the San Juans. The U.S. commission made it clear that it believed satisfactory negotiation could still be made with the Utes. On June 20, 1873, Felix R. Brunot and Nathan Bishop were named to renew negotiations leading to accession. Instructions to the commission were clear:

General Charles Adams replaced the weird Trask as the Los Pinos agent. Ouray considered Adams to be a good and trusted friend, even though he was the other brother-in-law (Agent James Thompson being the first) of Governor McCook, who was violently anti-Indian. Adams did seem to be truthful and honest in his dealings with the Utes. He eventually brought up the idea of trying to find Ouray's lost son as a means of getting Ouray to persuade the other Indians to enter into the Treaty of 1873. Adams wrote that he saw "the great superiority of Chief Ouray, his unconditional advice of peace under any circumstances, his eloquence and great influence over his tribe." (Denver Public Library)

The reservation is unnecessarily large, comprising upwards of 14 million acres of the best agricultural and mineral lands in Colorado. The number of Indians occupying it is comparatively small, not exceeding four or five thousand. The people of Colorado desire to have that portion of the Reserve not needed for Indian purposes thrown open to entry and settlement as public land in order that the agricultural and mineral resources may be developed—especially the portion lying between the southern boundary and the 38th degree of north latitude.

Brunot struck on trying to find Chief Ouray's lost son as a means of securing approval of the treaty. He wrote most of the nearby Indian agents and learned that the boy had gone from the Sioux to Neva, brother of Chief Friday of the Northern Arapaho, and then to the Southern Arapaho when Neva died. On June 25, 1873, Brunot and Indian agent Charles Adams had a secret meeting with Ouray in Cheyenne, Wyoming, where Brunot told Ouray of his efforts. Ouray was interested and made a proposition: "The Government is strong and can do what it wants; if the Government will do what it can for me and get my boy, I will do what I can for the Government in regard to our lands."

In July, several Yampa Ute women and children were killed by whites near Rawlins, Wyoming. It was only with great persuasion that Ouray kept the young men from retaliating. The Utes were eventually told to come to another council at Los Pinos about the middle of August, 1873, at which time Ouray's son would be delivered. Ouray requested that none of the Colorado government's people be present and that only Brunot serve as negotiator. Only those immediately concerned were to be admitted. It was hoped that these actions would keep the meeting as calm as possible.

Brunot and his secretary waited in Denver until September 1, but when they received no word from the messenger sent to get Ouray's boy, they started for Los Pinos anyway and reached the agency on September 5, 1873. Although Brunot had used every effort, he had failed to bring the boy to Los Pinos with him. Eighteen hundred Utes had been at Los Pinos for almost a month, and it was time for them to go on their hunt for the winter's food supply. Prospectors were flooding into the San Juans without permission. It was a powder keg situation. However, Brunot convinced Ouray that every effort had been used to get the boy, but that he was eluding the Indian agents. Brunot felt that the Arapahos were hiding the boy in Indian Territory, and he promised to keep up the search.

The council began the morning of September 6, 1873. Those in attendance included Felix Brunot, Thomas Cree (his secretary), Dr. James Phillips of Washington (Spanish interpreter for the commission), John Lawrence and James Fullerton (Spanish interpreters for the Indians), agent Charles Adams and Thomas Dolan (subagent at Tierra Amarilla). Ouray served as interpreter from Ute to Spanish.

Brunot opened with a prayer which Ouray interpreted for the Utes:

> Whenever we hold a council with the Indians, we know the Great Spirit sees us and knows our hearts, and we want to ask him to make our hearts alright and direct us in this council. I want you all to stand up while I talk to the Great Spirit.

Then Brunot had the audacity to tell the Utes how pleased he had been with their attitude the year before! He said he had urged the President to force the miners off the reservation, but had later heard that the Indians wanted to sell their land and thought that the miners' expulsion would only make trouble between Indians and whites. Thus this meeting had been called to determine whether the Indians really wanted to sell.

The Utes began by voicing complaints that the south and east boundaries of the reservation as defined in the Treaty of 1868 were not according to their understanding. Shavano, a Tabeguache chief, claimed that the lines the surveyors were running on the reservation were not according to the treaty. He said the mountains were the boundary of the reservation on the east and wanted to know what treaty had been made that gave the surveyors the privilege of coming in and running new lines. Since only latitude and longitude lines had been mentioned in the treaty, it was obvious the Utes hadn't understood what they had signed. Brunot replied that the way the whites have of telling lines is by the compass, which the Utes do not understand. When the treaty was made, the lines were named, but they were not put on the land. He said that the surveyors only wished to find out if the lines were where the Utes thought they were.

Ouray replied:

> They are measuring, and whenever they find a mine, they take a little piece more of our country. I interpreted it to the Utes when the treaty was made that the line would be from the Rio Grande to the head of the mountains. We understood it so until the present time. The rivers that run to the east from the mountain range are off the Reservation; those that run west are on it. The miners have come to San Juan and Washington Gulch, and the miners will gradually settle down on the lands in the valleys.

But, on the second day of the council (September 8), Ouray declared:

> We want you should tell Governor Elbert and the people in the Territory, that we are well pleased and perfectly satisfied with everything that has been done. Perhaps some of the people will not like it because we did not wish to sell our valley and farming lands, but we think we had good reason for not doing

This photograph evidently was made in Washington on the occasion of the treaty negotiations of 1880, but everyone in the picture also participated in the treaties of 1868 and 1873. Chief Ouray is, of course, seated in the center front of the picture. The four subchiefs are, from left to right, Warency, Shavano, Ankatosh and Guero, who were all loyal friends of Ouray. The United States government preferred to deal with Ouray rather than any of these friends, in part because they were all war chiefs who tended to be hotheaded and unwilling to work with the whites. (Colorado Historical Society)

From left to right in the back row of this photograph, which was taken in 1874, are Washington (a leading, but half-crazy Northern Ute chief), Susan (sister of Ouray), Johnson No. 2 (Susan's husband), Captain Jack (leader of the Thornburgh attack five years later), and John. In the middle row, in the same order, are Uriah Curtis (first interpreter for the Northern Utes), J.B. Thompson (agent at the Denver agency), Charles Adams (agent at the Los Pinos agency), and Otto Mears (probably also serving as an interpreter on this occasion). In the front row are Guero (Ute war chief), Chipeta, Ouray and Piah (Chipeta's brother.) (Colorado Historical Society)

so. We expect to occupy them ourselves before long for farming and stock raising. About eighty of our tribe are now raising corn and wheat, and we know not how soon we shall have to depend on ourselves for our bread. We do not want to sell our valley and farming lands for another reason. We know if we should the whites would go on them, build their cabins and drive in their stock, which would of course stray upon our lands, and then the whites themselves would crowd upon us till there would be trouble. We have many friends among the people, and want to live at peace and on good terms with them, and we feel that it would be better for all parties for a mountain range to be between us. We are perfectly willing to sell our mountain lands, and hope the miners will find heaps of gold and silver. We have no wish to molest or make them any trouble. We do not want they should go down into our valleys, however, and kill or scare away our game. We expect there will be much talk among the people and in the papers, about what we have done, and we hope you will let the people know how we feel about it.

Brunot replied that he knew Congress wanted not just the tops of the mountains but adjoining areas and wouldn't approve such a treaty. Ouray replied that the Utes "want security that the miners will not go any further." When Brunot indicated he didn't know if he could stop them, Ouray again responded: "Why cannot you stop them; is not the Government strong enough to keep its agreements with us?"

The main discussion then shifted to where the Southern Utes were going to live because they had technically been living off the reservation. It was agreed that Curecanti should go to Washington and talk personally with the President. Brunot said, "I have done the best I can for you. It is all over and we part good friends and we may as well adjourn the council."

Sidney Jocknick wrote of what happened next:

> The Commissioner's patience was well-nigh worn out at the obduracy of the Indians, but at the eleventh hour General Adams suggested to Mr. Brunot that it might be advantageous to interview Otto Mears. Accordingly Mr. Brunot went to Saguache to get his assistance. Mr. Mears told Mr. Brunot that if he would return to Los Pinos agency he would go with him. Mr. Mears got the Indians to sign the treaty. When they arrived at the agency Mr. Mears told Mr. Brunot that if he approved of it he would offer a nice gift to Chief Ouray—Indians being just as susceptible as the whites or blacks—and proposed to give Ouray a thousand-dollar salary for ten years. Mr. Brunot got rather indignant at this proposition, saying that the Government could not afford to bribe anybody. Mr. Mears insisted that it was not a bribe, but a salary. He then suggested to Ouray that he was getting old and, being chief, ought to have an income so that he could live without hunting and selling buckskin, and that the Government would agree to pay the Indians the interest on half a million dollars and himself a salary of one thousand dollars a year...
>
> Ouray being duly civilized and thrifty, accepted the proposition and signed the treaty which opened the San Juan mining region.

Brunot also brought up the fact that he was still trying to find

Ouray's son. Ouray, although disappointed, felt that Brunot had kept his word. It also was becoming very obvious that the whites were going to move into the San Juans with or without a treaty. And perhaps the "bribe" did have some effect. On September 13, 1873, the treaty was signed. Actually, there was no longer a "treaty" as such since treaties with Indians were forbidden by United States law after 1871. A "treaty" was made by the U.S. Senate with foreign powers. The federal government felt that the Indians no longer held the position of a foreign power—they had lost their sovereignty to the United States. In the future there were to be only "agreements" with the Indians (though still commonly referred to as treaties), and these were to be ratified by act of the entire Congress, not just the Senate, and then signed by the President.

The Utes ceded the entire San Juan area, which included most of present day Ouray, San Juan, Hinsdale, Archuleta, Dolores, La Plata, Montezuma and San Miguel counties. The chiefs of all seven Ute bands agreed to the treaty. Ouray was even able to get three-fourths of all of the Utes to ratify the agreement! The treaty was later approved by the U.S. Senate on April 29, 1874, and was subsequently ratified by the House of Representatives and the President.

The Indians had accepted the treaty on the condition that representatives of the different Indian bands, along with Thomas Cree, Thomas Dolan, and agent Charles Adams, would visit the area of the proposed sale. If they found the land "to be mining and not farming land," then all the Indians would sign it; if, however, it was farming land, then the agreement would be invalid.

The $25,000 per year paid for the land worked out to about seven and a half cents per acre at a time when the United States government was charging homesteaders $1.25 per acre for less valuable land. An agency was to be built in the southern part of the reservation for the Weeminuche, Mouache and Capote bands. The treaty expressly reaffirmed that part of the 1868 treaty which provided that no person except officers, agents, or employees of the government should ever be permitted to pass over, settle or reside on the Ute land. It also said that the Utes could continue to hunt on the land ceded—and that Ouray would receive $1,000 per year for the rest of his life.

In accordance with the agreement made, Cree, Charles Adams, Thomas Dolan and representatives from the different tribes visited the area in question. They saw many mines being developed. One mine with considerable money invested was said to yield $1,000 per day. Some $500 to $600 per ton veins had been located, and between 250 and 300 miners were residing in the country. The Indians were convinced that the land they saw was mining land and ratified the treaty. However, they did not by any means see all of the area proposed to be ceded.

Indian agent Charles Adams wrote to **The Rocky Mountain News** on October 1, 1873, reporting that the Utes had ceded "the San

Several of the participants in the treaty negotiations of 1872 are in this picture, probably taken shortly after the conference ended in failure. In the front row (from left to right) are Wanztiz; James B. Thompson, special agent in Denver; and Hondo. In the back row are J.S. Littlefield, Indian agent at White River; Tab-n-cha-kot; Pah-ant; Catz; and U.M. Curtis, the official interpreter at the meetings. The Utes were adamant that they were not going to give up any more of their land and that they couldn't understand why the white man would not enforce the treaties he had already made. The whites tried to convince the Utes that the prospectors and miners would come anyway, but Ouray asked why the United States wasn't strong enough to control its own people. (Colorado Historical Society)

Juan mining country and received ... $25,000 annually forever. It was hard work to overcome the stubbornness of the Indians and I am heartily glad that it has ended so well for all."

The Utes may have thought that the treaty was selling only the mines and retaining the valleys for agriculture, but the treaty itself referred to the 107th north latitude and the 38th parallel, with an exception that if Uncompahgre Park extended into the area given up, it was still to belong to the Utes.

Ouray received 160 acres of land with a comfortable house in addition to his salary. Sidney Jocknick said that Ouray didn't really care about the money, and that he took it as:

> ...an offset to the loss of dignity which was the penalty he paid for exercising "a straw-boss's authority" over his subjects ...

Ouray was so entirely devoted to Chipeta that his

acceptance of a salary was due alone to the promptings of a conscientious desire to generously provide for her, in order that in case of his untimely death at the hands of his enemies, she would never have to suffer from poverty in her old age.

For once the whites apparently kept their word on at least part of the agreement. A seventeen-year-old boy named Friday was found and brought with a delegation of Arapahos led by Powder Face to Washington. Brunot arranged for Ouray, Chipeta, agent Adams, T.A. Dolan, Otto Mears and a delegation of eight other Utes to also come in October, 1873, a month after the signing of the treaty so that the two enemy tribes might try to make peace as well. Brunot in fact argued eloquently that the two tribes *had* to make peace.

The meeting turned out to be a real verbal sparring match between Powder Face, Friday and Ouray. At the meeting, Friday wanted to know what his name was in Ute. Ouray asked if he did not know it. One of the other Utes went up to Friday and said that they were cousins and that when they had played together as boys, they had called him "Cotoan." Brunot interjected that if Friday didn't want to go back to Ouray, then Ouray didn't want him to go. To this, Friday said that he could not understand the Utes and wished to stay with the Arapahos. Ouray asked if someone knew about the fight at which Friday was taken, and Powder Face responded that the Northern Arapahos had captured him, but that Friday himself knew about the circumstances. Friday wanted the Utes to disclose the location where he had been lost to see if they truly knew the place. Ouray said his son had been in a fight about thirty miles above Denver, but Powder Face responded that Friday had been taken during a fight further to the north and that the captured young man Ouray referred to was actually at the boy's home now. Commissioner Brunot asked, "How far north was Friday captured?" and Powder Face said "Just the other side of the Rocky Mountains." The following conversation ensued:

Ouray: The whites have tried to have me get this boy. But he is not my boy. If he was he would not talk that way. Would speak differently.

Commissioner: Ouray don't want the boy if he is not his. But we would like to find out about the other boy. Now is there anything more you want to say about peace? Ask Ouray if he will speak.

Ouray: They acknowledge hunting Utes. The Utes never hunt the Arapahos. They come to hunt the Utes, and we have nothing to say to them. We let them alone. But we must defend ourselves.

Commissioner: I would like Powder Face to say if that is true, that the Utes never come to fight the Arapahos but the Arapahos always go to fight the Utes.

Powder Face: That is true.

Commissioner: Then I have something to say. Whether you make a peace with the Utes or not and are ever found off your reservation fighting Utes, Government will send soldiers to punish you. And if it don't send enough the first time it will send more. These Utes are at peace with the government and it is bound to protect them.

Nothing was said about the forked scar which would have definitely proven the boy as Ouray's son. It was noted that Friday was left handed as was Paron. Brunot however later stated that anyone who had seen the two together would have immediately recognized them to be father and son because of a remarkable resemblance. Ouray later said that he didn't feel the United States had tried that hard to get his son back. However, he may have made this statement because his attitude towards the whites was beginning to harden. Friday returned to the Arapahos where he spent the rest of his life.

The Brunot Treaty provided an uneasy truce. The Utes resented the white man being in the San Juans, and not all of them were willing to sign the treaty. The whites were scared because the Ute reservation surrounded the San Juans on three sides. Furthermore, the whites (especially cattlemen) were violating the Treaty of 1873 by continuously trespassing on the Southern Ute reservation. A Ute delegation, led by Ouray, along with the commissioners, marked the boundaries of the treaty. William H. Jackson described one of these boundary trees in his diary, which he said was personally marked by Ouray. He remarked that the Indians were running settlers away that were trying to locate outside the purchase. Almost from the day it was agreed to, it was obvious that the Treaty of 1873 was not going to work!

Chapter Seven

ALFERD PACKER— THE MAN-EATER

Colorado's famous cannibal story involves Chief Ouray not as a "savage" participant but as an interested onlooker. Ouray became a part of the incident both at its beginning and at its end, and the story is worth telling once again.

In early November of 1873, a group of twenty-one men planned to travel from Bingham, Utah, to Breckenridge, Colorado. A big gold strike had been rumored and the men were anxious to leave. However, none of the group had ever been through the territory and they needed a guide. Alferd Packer offered to lead them, but most of the men were skeptical because he didn't look like he could be trusted. In fact, Packer had been jailed a short time before in Salt Lake City for passing counterfeit money. But the prospectors were eager to head for Breckenridge, and they chose Packer as a guide since he was the only one who said he knew the area.

The group left Bingham on November 8, 1873, but progress was slow and difficult. Then on January 21, 1874, a calamity occurred: their raft overturned in midstream while they were crossing the Green River and most of their food supply was swept away. It was already evident that the winter was going to be harsh, but they wrongly assumed that they would still be able to supplement their meager supplies with game along the route. The group's provisions soon ran out, but they struggled on, eating rabbits and the oats they had brought along for the horses.

Packer's group passed what is now the Colorado-Utah border about January 25, 1874, and camped on the south side of the Grand River (now called the Colorado) near the site of present day Grand Junction. Three Utes stumbled upon the party and, when asked, told the prospectors of Chief Ouray's whereabouts, a three day's journey away. Around the first of February, Packer's half-starved band reached Ouray's winter camp near present day Montrose. They had traveled a little more than three hundred miles in two-and a-half months, an average of only about four miles a day. All of the Packer group arrived safely, although hungry.

After Ouray was sure that the men passing through his territory were only prospectors they were welcomed warmly, even though they were trespassing on the Ute reservation, and the government only a few months earlier had promised to keep all white men, except United States employees, out. Ouray and his band fed the

When Chief Ouray agreed to sit for this picture for William Henry Jackson, it encouraged the other Utes at the Los Pinos agency to do the same. Jackson was, of course, working with a portable studio and evidently tacked white canvas onto a wall and spread what is probably a black blanket on the ground or floor to make this look like a studio shot. Ouray is wearing finely beaded moccasins and a beaded shirt that were more than likely made by Chipeta, who excelled at this type of work. This picture, and the one of Chipeta that follows, were taken only a few months after the Packer affair. (Colorado Historical Society)

William H. Jackson also photographed "the young and comely Chipeta" at Los Pinos in 1874. Evidently, the black blanket used in Ouray's photo contrasted too much with Chipeta's fine white buckskin skirt, so Jackson laid white canvas or cloth over it. The folds in this cloth, and in the one on the wall behind Ouray and Chipeta, are easily seen in this photograph. Chipeta also wears a blanket shawl and several pieces of fine jewelry, but her plain moccasins were more commonly worn by the Utes than the ones that Ouray has on. (Colorado Historical Society)

prospectors until they returned to full health, and Ouray visited them almost daily.

Ouray warned the group not to proceed any further because of heavy snows that were already piled deep in the high mountains, and even helped the prospectors set up permanent camps where they could stay until spring. Most of the group took his advice, but soon some of the prospectors became anxious to leave. Ouray again strongly recommended that they stay put for the winter, but O.S. Loutsenhizer and four other men soon left in spite of the admonitions. Packer offered to guide the group to a shortcut but was quickly refused. The men soon became separated and wandered aimlessly. Two of them found an emaciated cow that was part of the Los Pinos herd and killed it with jackknives, then made it to the Los Pinos cow camp. James Kelley and Sidney Jocknick went out with a sled full of provisions and rescued the other three. The five men spent three weeks at the cow camp, then forged on to Los Pinos and Saguache.

Later, six others at Ouray's camp—Packer, Shannon Wilson Bell, Israel Swan, George Noon (a sixteen-year-old boy), Frank Miller and James Humphreys—decided they would also try to make it to the Los Pinos cow camp or to Saguache. Once again, Ouray protested, saying he felt sure the first group was already dead in the mountains and that not one of his Indians would go as a guide. However, when convinced that they were going to leave, Ouray tried to tell the group the route and even drew a rough map. The six left about February 9, ignoring Ouray's very specific advice to always keep sight of the Gunnison River and to go to the Los Pinos cow camp, get supplies, and only then go over to Saguache. All of the rest of the original prospecting party stayed with Ouray until spring, sharing his food and hospitality.

Even after all the warnings, Packer decided to take the shortcut over the mountains directly to Saguache. Within three days the group was in trouble. By the time the group made it to near present day Lake City, they were lost, freezing, and starving. Nighttime temperatures were going to forty below. For almost two months, the party was not heard from.

Alonzo Hartman, an employee at the Ute cow camp near Gunnison, first saw Packer come back into civilization. He later testified in court:

> There was no one in the section nearer than fifty miles, so it seemed strange that a man should drop down from nowhere so suddenly. I was wondering what it all meant when he came up.
>
> "Hello," I said. "Are you lost?"
>
> Packer, for that was who it was, rubbed his eyes. "Is this the agency?" he said.
>
> I told him it was. He didn't seem different from any other man who had been exposed to winter weather.

His hair and beard were long and matted; but he showed little sign of having suffered from severe winter weather, lost in a wild uninhabited country with the thermometer showing between thirty and fifty degrees below zero many mornings. Naturally, one would expect that no man could stand the exposure this man had been through and live; but here was the man alive and seemingly none the worse for his experiences.

About mid-April, Packer went to the Los Pinos agency, where he told Stephen A. Dole (who was in charge of the agency in General Adams' absence), James Downer, and Herman Lauter that after he left Ouray's camp, he had hurt his leg and was unable to walk. He said that he became separated from the rest of his party, which had not desired to be held up by a crippled man, and that he had wandered around for months with no food other than berries, rabbits and squirrels. The others were presumed to have gone to the Silverton area. Packer's story was not an uncommon one for the mountains and was generally accepted.

After sympathizing with Packer for all the hardships that he had undergone, Dole offered him a job. Packer refused but sold a Winchester rifle to Downer for ten dollars. He then left for Saguache, which was forty-five miles away. He said he had had his fill of Colorado and wanted to return to his home in Pennsylvania.

Packer stayed for six days in Saguache with Larry Dolan, an Irish saloonkeeper. Dolan was surprised that the newcomer occasionally displayed comparatively large sums of money. Packer spent most of his time in Saguache drinking and playing poker. Soon after his arrival, he met various persons from the original group of twenty-one prospectors who had waited until spring and had easily made the journey in April without mishap. Chief Ouray was supposed to have also met Packer during this time in Saguache and to have commented that Packer appeared to be in "extremely good shape" for the hardships he said he endured.

During his stay in Saguache, Packer went to Otto Mears' store and bought a horse for seventy dollars, paying the money in bank notes. Mears had been told that Packer had been jailed for passing counterfeit money, so he refused one of the notes which looked like it could be counterfeit. Packer then pulled out another pocketbook and took from it another note, which Mears accepted. However, Mears thought it quite strange that Packer had two pocketbooks. The members of the original party also began to suspect Packer when they discovered that he had much more money in Saguache than when he left Bingham. Once, when drunk, he had been seen with several items which were known to have belonged to the missing men, none of whom had been heard from.

Six days after Packer reached Saguache, General Adams stopped in at Mears' store en route to the Los Pinos agency from Denver. Mears and several of the members of the original party related their

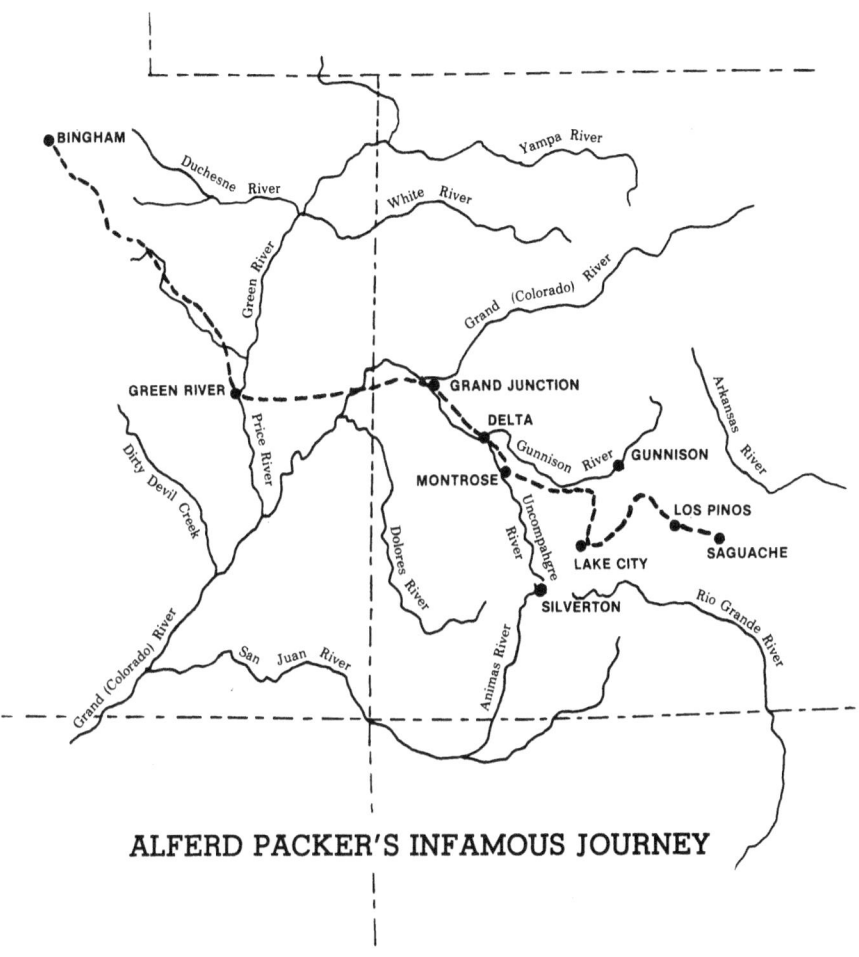

ALFERD PACKER'S INFAMOUS JOURNEY

Alferd Packer and his group left Bingham, Utah Territory, on November 8, 1873, headed towards Breckenridge in the Territory of Colorado. On January 21, 1874, the party's raft overturned on the Green River and most of their food was lost. They were found by the Utes half-starved near present day Grand Junction and were taken to Chief Ouray's winter camp in the Delta-Montrose area. After resting up, Packer and others attempted to go to Saguache. Ouray warned them to keep the Gunnison River in sight at all times, but the group turned south and followed the Lake Fork of the Gunnison to near present day Lake City. It was here that Packer's grizzly tale begins. Several months later, he came into the Los Pinos agency looking none the worse for his ordeal, and though the story has been told many times, no one may ever know what really happened in between.

Alonzo Hartman was in charge of the government herd of cattle which was kept for distribution to the Indians at the Los Pinos agency at Cochetopa. When Alferd Packer came in from his infamous journey, it was Hartman, who had spent that winter at the agency proper, that first saw him. Hartman testified at Packer's trial that Packer seemed "none the worse for his experiences." Hartman helped transfer the government herd to Cow Creek at the Uncompahgre agency, but afterwards returned to the Gunnison location, where he acquired title to the old government cow camp cabin and corrals, for which the government had no further use. Here he began his own cattle business, developing his Dos Rios Ranch and eventually becoming wealthy. (Denver Public Library)

suspicions to Adams. Adams decided he would try to talk Packer into going to the Los Pinos agency so that Adams would have jurisdiction over him and either force a confession or hold Packer prisoner until a full investigation could be made. Adams told Packer that if he would act as a guide, a search party would be outfitted at the agency to look for the missing men. At first Packer gave many excuses for not going, but finally he consented and went back to the agency, accompanied by Mears and several members of the original party.

When they reached the agency, Adams confronted Packer and told him that they suspected him of killing his companions. He asked where Packer had gotten the large sums of money he had been spending in Saguache. Packer swore he borrowed the money from a friend, but he couldn't give the friend's name. Packer finally told Adams that his five companions had died from hunger and exposure at various points in the journey, and that, since burial was impossible because of the frozen ground, their bodies were left where they had died. General Adams asked about the strips of human flesh which the Indians had found along Packer's trail. Packer continued to be evasive, and having no ready explanations, he was jailed.

On May 8, 1874, Packer finally made a confession:

> Old man Swan died first and was eaten by the other five persons, about ten days out of camp. Four or five days afterwards Humphreys died and was also eaten; he had about one hundred and thirty three dollars ($133). I found the pocketbook and took the money. Some time afterwards, while I was carrying wood, the butcher was killed—as the other two told me, accidentally—and he was also eaten. Bell shot "California" with Swan's gun and I killed Bell. Shot him, I covered up the remains and took a large piece along. Then traveled fourteen days into the agency. Bell wanted to kill me with his rifle—struck a tree and broke his gun.

In June of 1874, J.A. Randolph, a photographer for **Harper's Weekly**, found the bodies of the five men two-and-a-half miles southeast of present day Lake City. All of the men were close together, their skulls crushed with a hatchet. Bell had been shot in the back. A crude cabin was nearby.

On August 8, 1874, someone gave Packer a key and he escaped from the Saguache jail. It wasn't until March 11, 1883, that Jean "Frenchy" Cabazon, one of the members of the original party of twenty-one, recognized Packer's unusually high-pitched voice in a hotel in Fort Fetterman, Wyoming, and Packer was recaptured. Packer had been using the assumed name of John Swartze. On March 16, 1883, Packer made a second confession to General Adams, giving a different version of the events:

> When we left Ouray's camp we had about seven

In June of 1874, J.A. Randolph, a photographer for "Harper's Weekly Magazine," discovered the remains of Packer's victims about two-and-a-half miles away from Lake City on what is now called Cannibal Plateau. This sketch was published by the magazine on October 17, 1874. The artist has written names next to each of the victims, but one must wonder how he could have positively identified them all; according to every version of the killing, the victims were not this close together, so the artist obviously took some liberties. The discovery of the bodies discredited Packer's story that the men had been killed one by one at various locations by the other men in the party. (Colorado Historical Society)

days food for one man, we traveled two or three days and it came a storm ... all the men were crying and one of them was crazy. Swan asked me to go up and find out whether I could see something from the mountains ... When I came back to camp after being gone nearly all day I found the red headed man (Bell) who acted crazy in the morning sitting near the fire roasting a piece of meat which he had cut out of the leg of the German butcher (Miller). The latter's body was lying the furthest off from the fire, down the stream, his skull was crushed in with the hatchet. The other three men were lying near the fire, they were cut in the forehead with the hatchet, some had two, some three, cuts. I came within a rod of the fire, when the man saw me. He got up with his hatchet towards me

This photograph of Alferd Packer was taken about 1886. Packer's first trial in Lake City, which resulted in a verdict of guilty to a charge of first degree murder, was set aside by a later Colorado Supreme Court decision. The Court found that the Colorado legislature had not properly preserved the 1873 penalty for murder when it enacted the first laws of the new state in 1876. (Packer killed his victims in 1873.) Packer was tried the second time in Gunnison in 1886 and was found guilty of the reduced charge of manslaughter; he was sentenced to forty years in jail. (Colorado Historical Society)

when I shot him sideways through the belly. He fell on his face, the hatchet fell forward, I grabbed it and hit him in the top of the head ...

Packer stood trial between April 6 and April 13, 1883, in Lake City, Colorado, almost exactly ten years after the crime. He took the stand in his own defense and spent six hours describing the events as in his second confession. The jury, nevertheless, found him guilty after deliberating for three hours. Melvin B. Gerry, a Democrat in a highly Republican county, sentenced him with some of the most eloquent words ever used by a trial judge:

> A jury of twelve honest citizens of the county have sat in judgment on your case and upon their oaths they find you guilty of wilful and premeditated murder—a murder revolting in all its details ... Whether your murderous hand was guided by the misty light of the moon, or the flickering blaze of the campfire, you only can tell. No eye saw the bloody deed performed; nor ear save your own caught the groans of your dying victims. You then and there robbed the living of life and then robbed the dead of the reward of honest toil which they had accumulated, at least so say the jury...
>
> Society cannot forgive you for the crime you have committed. It enforces the old Mosaic law of a life for a life, and your life must be taken as the penalty of your crime. I am but the instrument of society to impose the punishment which the law provides. While society cannot forgive, it will forget. As the days come and go and the years of our pilgrimage roll by, the memory of you and your crimes will fade from the minds of men.
>
> With God it is different. He will not forget, but will forgive. He pardoned the dying thief on the cross. He is the same God today as then—A God of love and of mercy, of long suffering and kind forbearance; a God who tempers the wind to the shorn lamb and promises rest to all the weary and heartbroken children of men; and it is to this God I commend you.

But rather than this thoughtful and carefully worded judgment, Judge M.B. Gerry went down in history as having said:

> There was seven Democrats in Hinsdale County and you ate five of them, damn you. I sentence you to hang by the neck until dead, dead, dead, as a warning against reducing the Democratic population of the state.

Packer was sentenced to death, but the Colorado Supreme Court later reversed all murder cases prior to 1876 under the technicality that when Colorado became a state, the laws were not enacted in such a way as to include a murder which happened when Colorado was a territory. The Court perhaps also felt that the highly prejudicial articles about Packer published all over the state at the time he was tried made a fair trial impossible. Packer was ordered back into court, this time in Gunnison, to be retried on manslaughter charges. The new trial took place between August 2 and August 5,

This is a prison "mug shot" of the convicted "man-eater." After serving less than fifteen years of his forty-year prison sentence, Alferd Packer was reluctantly pardoned by Colorado Governor Thomas, who resigned almost immediately afterwards. Packer spent most of his remaining years in and around Denver because he was forbidden to leave the state. He is buried in the Littleton cemetery. Colorado's skid-row parson, Bishop Rice, accompanied by several assistants, once paid a visit to his grave; they brought with them a goat, into which they "transferred his sins." Purportedly, Packer's soul would then be released to go to Paradise. (Colorado Historical Society)

1886. This time the jury deliberated only two-and-a-half hours; Packer was found guilty and sentenced to forty years in the penitentiary (eight years for each of the five men).

After spending fifteen years in the State Penitentiary at Canon City, Packer was paroled by Governor Charles Thomas in January, 1901. He died in Littleton, Colorado, in January, 1911, at the age of sixty-five. Several college and governmental cafeterias now bear his name.

Chapter Eight

LOS PINOS II—
THE UNCOMPAHGRE AGENCY

The Los Pinos agency wasn't working out. Because of its location at almost ten thousand feet above sea level, the Utes only stayed there for three or four months in the summer, and they received little training in agriculture or education. As mentioned earlier, the agency was not even technically in Ute territory by some ten or twenty miles, and it was hard to get the Indians' supplies to them.

Ouray wanted a new agency, and preferred the Gunnison area because he was not sure that the Indians would go any farther. The Cebolla Valley between present day Gunnison and Sapinero was another site possibility. But finally, the Uncompahgre Valley was chosen. The new agency was to be located eleven miles south of present day Montrose, near what is now Colona. The new cattle camp was to be on Cow Creek, another seven miles to the south. The government felt it could keep a closer eye on the miners and the Utes from this new location.

The move to the new site began in the summer of 1875. Quite a bit is known about the move and the establishment of the new agency, thanks to Sidney Jocknick, a cowboy for the agency. He wrote at length of his experiences in his book, **Early Days on the Western Slope of Colorado.**

Shortly before the move to the new agency, it was discovered that Adams was a Catholic instead of a Unitarian. The Unitarians demanded another agent (although Adams was obviously doing a good job). He was removed, and Henry F. Bond, a Harvard graduate, was appointed to replace him. One very well-documented account of the Utes and Ouray occurred during Bond's short tenure when William Jackson, the famous frontier photographer, came to the agency at Los Pinos. Jackson was traveling with the Hayden survey party which was intruding into Ute territory. One of Jackson's objectives was to be at the Los Pinos agency during an annuity distribution so that he could photograph the Indians. In August of 1873, the survey party came upon some sixty or seventy tepees spread out over a mile on Cochetopa Pass. All the grazing land in sight was covered with Ute ponies. Agent Bond was crestfallen when he discovered that Jackson had primarily come to photograph the Indians rather than Bond himself.

In his autobiography, **Time Exposure,** Jackson wrote about the Los Pinos agency and Ouray:

William Henry Jackson evidently took this self portrait in 1874, the same year he was part of the Hayden Survey, which visited Los Pinos. He was already a seasoned adventurer, having made his way to California as a bullwhacker on a wagon train and then driving a herd of wild horses back to Omaha. It was there that he bought his first photographic equipment with a small down payment, making installments on the balance as business warranted. The vast number of pictures that Jackson took during his lifetime eventually grew to more than forty thousand negatives. (Denver Public Library)

Of all the Indians I have known Ouray was quite the most extraordinary. Some forty years of age, he was, unlike the majority of his fellow tribesmen, short and rather dumpy. His head, while uncommonly large, was well formed; his features were regular and well modeled; his teeth were white and fine. Most striking, his expression was indicative not only of good will but of great intelligence. Ouray was a lover of peace, and his career was unblemished by a single instance of violence against the whites. His personal life was equally blameless. Ouray dwelt austerely with his life; he used no tobacco, and he hated whisky. Before he died, in fact, Ouray joined the Methodist Church!

We talked together until noon, and our conversation was carried on in English with the greatest ease. Among his other virtues and accomplishments, Ouray included the gift of languages. On several occasions he had been taken to Washington to act as interpreter and it was largely for that service that the Government had built him his house and given him an annual pension of $1,000. Ouray not only dwelt in a house like his paleface brothers but, by preference, wore their clothes—a black broadcloth suit, polished boots and a derby hat.

After dinner Jackson set up his camera on the porch of the agent's house and took pictures of Mr. and Mrs. Bond, Ouray (now in beaded ceremonial buckskin), and Chipeta.

Ernest Ingersoll, who accompanied Jackson, also wrote of Ouray and Chipeta:

Ouray ordinarily wore a civilized dress of black broadcloth, and even boots, though he had never cut off his long hair, which he still bound up in two queues, Indian fashion. But now he came out in buckskin costume of native cut, full and flowing, with long fringes trailing from his arms and shoulders, skirts and leggings, until they dragged upon the ground.

These garments were beaded in the most profuse and expensive manner; and as he gravely strode through the circle of spectators and seated himself in a dignified and proud way, his many medals flashing, he looked every inch a monarch.

His wife (Chipeta) was that day about the most prepossessing Indian woman I ever saw, and Ouray was immensely proud of her. She evidently had prepared with great care for this event, yet at the last was very timid about taking her place before the camera; but the encouragement of her husband and assistance of Mrs. Bond, soon overcame her scruples, and she sat down as full of dimpling smiles as the veriest bride. The doeskin of which her dress was made was almost as white as cotton, and nearly as soft as silk. From every edge and seam hung thick white fringes, twelve or fifteen inches long, while a pretty trimming of bead work and porcupine-quill embroidery set off a costume which cost Ouray not less than $125.

Jackson had to suspend operations early that day because a storm came up. The next day, something had happened, and most of the Indians refused to have their pictures taken. Evidently Guero and some of the more conservative leaders of the tribe had prevailed over Chief Ouray. On the other hand, Chief Tush-a-qui-not, or "Piah" (another brother of Chipeta's) took no strong position: after Jackson acquired two or three Navajo blankets and Piah agreed to pose. He was a superb subject. After taking a few pictures of Piah and his family in front of their tepee, Jackson was forced once again by bad weather to put his camera away. By the following day, even Piah had turned against him. No one would pose, nor would they permit Jackson to use his camera even from a distance. After three or four more days of organized opposition, Jackson gave up and moved on.

Shortly after Jackson's visit, the agency was moved to its new spot on the Uncompahgre River. Hundreds of Indian ponies were used to make the initial trip. Later—in a journey that took three weeks and required twelve men, four wagons, twelve yoke of oxen, and a mule team—the sawmill was transported to a new location. Twelve hundred head of cows were eventually moved from Taylor Park which is north of present day Gunnison. Jocknick and five other men immediately built a cabin and corral upon their arrival. Alonzo Hartman, one of the men who made the move, later reported that "it was no small task to move all the agency stuff over seventy-five miles of mountains and deep canons with herds of cattle and sheep and hundreds of ponies, part of them packed heavily with Ute belongings." The Utes brought dogs, tepees, wagons and thousands of possessions. The move was completed on November 20, 1875.

This is a sketch from a picture made by Jackson in 1874 while he was the official photographer for the Hayden expedition. Seated in the center of the photo is Dr. Ferdinand Vandeveer Hayden. Standing to the right is Ernest Ingersoll, who published many popular accounts of the expedition and the places they visited. These reports are now widely used and quoted by historians because of their vivid descriptions and beautiful language. Jackson himself is at the far right. Seated at the left is W.H. Holmes; behind him stands G.B. Chittendon. (Colorado Historical Society)

Piah, brother of Chipeta, posed with his peace medal for this picture by Jackson. Piah was not as peace-loving as Ouray. He often hung around with Colorow, threatening settlers, but he seemed to owe no allegiance to any one particular band of Utes. He slowly built up his own group of followers, who held the United States government in contempt. On more than one occasion, Piah wanted to give a scalp dance in Denver, using the still-fresh scalps of the Ute enemies. When he finally succeeded in doing so, the resulting scene was so revolting to the local populace that his actions became one of the main reasons the Denver agency was eventually closed. (Denver Public Library)

Henry Bond didn't last long as the new agent. A count of the government cattle driven from Gunnison showed a shortage of over two hundred head that had probably strayed back to the Taylor Park area and been taken by white men. The cowboys attempted to cover up the error by a recount that showed that all was okay. Ouray also charged that the agent was selling supplies and pocketing the money. Bond was requested to resign within a year of his appointment. Major W.D. Wheeler was appointed to succeed him and arrived at the agency in the fall of 1876. Wheeler, of course, was a member of the Unitarian Church. Although he was stern and exacting, he was highly respected by the employees and Indians alike.

The Uncompahgre agency (also called Los Pinos or Los Pinos II for quite some time) was used mainly in the winter by the Utes because they spent most of the summer in the mountains. The old Los Pinos agency was kept as a subagency from 1875 to 1879, when it was abandoned and the buildings sold.

Once the sawmill arrived, the new agency buildings began to go up quickly. Boards were cut, and work began on administrative offices, houses, and corrals. A flag pole was ordered, and a contract for 300,000 adobe bricks was given to some Mexican laborers so that the agent's home, his office, the post office, and other buildings could be constructed. Other structures included the physician's house, the carpenter's house, a blacksmith's shop, mess hall, the trader's house, a log barn, and a large log building for the farmer, miller, herder, and other laborers.

A six-room adobe house was built for Ouray about eight miles north of the new agency in return for the help he had given the United States government at the many treaty councils. Otto Mears was paid the generous sum of $10,000 as the contractor for the house. The dwelling was located just south of present day Montrose and included a fenced, five-hundred acre farm with about fifty acres cultivated in hay, grain, and vegetables. Most importantly it had one of the biggest and clearest springs in the area. Besides Ouray's house there were other buildings such as a storehouse, buildings for hired help, an outside kitchen, granaries, stables, and corrals. Ouray hired Mexican and Indian laborers and ran a herd of two hundred horses and mules on the property, as well as sheep, goats, and cattle.

His house was furnished with iron beds, rocking chairs, tables, chairs, rugs, stoves, and other often "uncomfortable" and "impractical" white man's furnishings. Chipeta even took on the burden of polishing silver and washing china. They owned a piano and had a Mexican servant who answered their silver bell and brought forth the horses and carriage. Ernest Ingersoll reported on this phase of Ouray's life:

> Here, Ouray, the fine old head-chief of the Ute confederation, lived toward the end of his life in a good

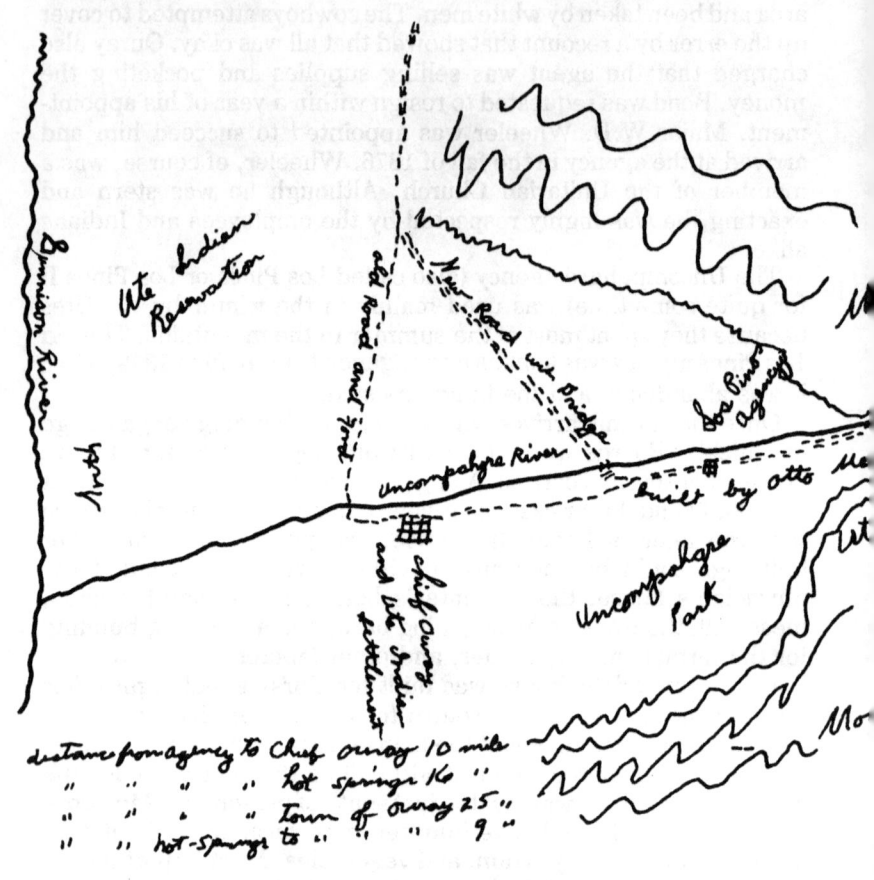

In 1878, agent Josiah Fogg drew this map as part of a report to his superiors. The 1873 treaty established the reservation line at ten miles north of the 38th parallel, which is about half a mile south of present day Ridgway, with the stipulation that Uncompahgre Park was to remain Ute territory even if it turned out to be beyond that line. The problem was that no one knew exactly where Uncompahgre Park ended. The park was important because it contained the Utes' sacred springs. In 1876, the four-mile square was added to Ute territory to solve the problem. The whites, however, wanted a large part of the square, since it was prime farmland, and they began moving into the area anyway. The map was drawn to help explain the situation to Washington.
(Courtesy of Centuries Research, Steve Baker)

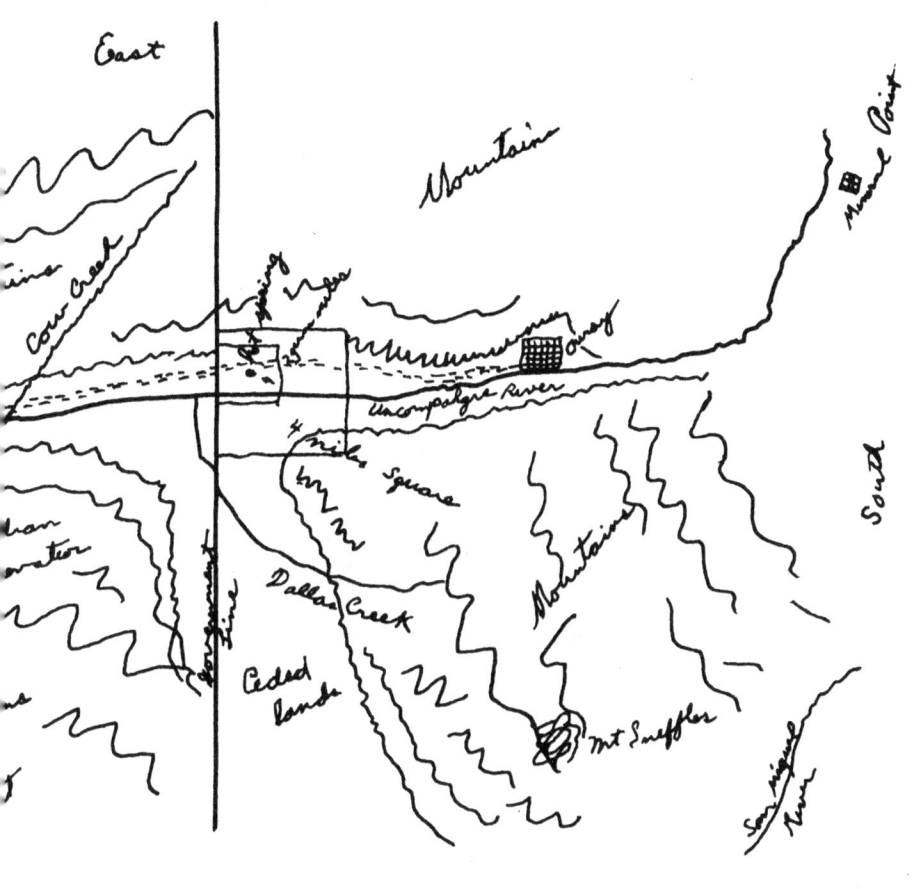

house built of adobe after the Mexican fashion, and cultivated neighboring bottom lands. His farm made the grand center of Ute interest, and from the pleasant groves near it radiated all the trails across mountain and plain. Many outhouses of log and frame surrounded the main building and testifying that order was one of the great chief's good qualities.

Ouray tried to set an example for his people. He felt that they had to augment their hunting with stock raising and farming because of their reduced territory. But the Utes scorned farming and did only fairly well as ranchers.

This is an artist's rendition of the second Los Pinos agency (also called the Uncompahgre agency), which was established in the autumn of 1875. The building in the background (A) is the agent's house. The storehouse (B) and the underground vegetable storage (D) were for supplies. The dwellings and mess hall for the Mexican employees are labeled (C). Chief Ouray's carriage (E) and freight wagons (F) were used for transportation. This drawing was for the October 25, 1879, edition of "Harper's Weekly." The artist must have drawn from a sketch, because most of the buildings were actually made from adobe, which is one reason why there were skilled Mexican laborers at the agency. The Mexicans also shared their farming expertise with the Utes. (Colorado Historical Society)

Ouray himself began to adopt many of the white man's ways (however not in the comic manner of many of his colleagues). He was trying to show his people how they could adjust to a new way of life. Edward McCook gave him a fancy carriage, and he loved to go for rides in it—he even had a hired Mexican driver. Ouray's Mexican servant, Mariano, lived with him and served as his private secretary. Ouray carried calling cards, had an ornate desk, and used the telegraph often. He had a refined and polished manner and loved to talk. If he had an honored guest, he would bring out wine and cigars. He even met with his chiefs in his dining room, which had only a table and one chair, where Ouray sat. The other chiefs sat on the floor.

For her part, Chipeta learned to play the guitar and had a beautiful singing voice. William Saunders, a reporter for the City of Ouray paper, wrote about his meeting with her at this time:

At the time this photo was taken, Chief Ouray's house near present day Montrose was already deserted. The cook's house and storage building are off to the left. The homestead was built by Otto Mears at a reputed cost of $10,000, which was a very large sum for the time. Ouray and Chipeta lived here between 1875 and 1880, trying to set an example as ranchers and farmers for the other Utes. Enough Indians did locate here that it became known as a Ute settlement. In 1944, the house burned, but a replica was subsequently built. Both the replica and the cook's house were eventually destroyed also. On August 15, 1956, the Ute Indian Museum of the Colorado Historical Society was dedicated on this site. (Colorado Historical Society)

Chipeta got used to my presence very soon, and gave free rein to her natural vivacity, talking in Spanish, mostly about two pets she had, a mountain lion and a deer, which she had trained to consort with each other on most friendly terms. Her voice was low and clear and melodious and she talked with a fascinating play of feature and gestures ... (Chipeta) rode like an Amazon and she and (her) horse might have been one, so perfectly did her body meet the movements of his. Her horse was a sorrel, a pony she told me she had raised herself, and he was that unusual horse, a natural single footer.

As time went on, Ouray became even more highly respected among the whites. Sidney Jocknick wrote:

Although one of the savages of North America, he

This portrait of Chief Ouray was made by William Chamberlain in the late 1870s, but was circulated under Jackson's name for years afterwards. Chamberlain was associated with Jackson's studio in Denver for a time, so Jackson may have had some legitimate claim to it. Ouray was once again dressed in white man's clothes including even studs and a watch fob. He was trying his best at this time to imitate the white man in every way possible, but by the time of his death, Ouray had reverted to his Indian dress and had pretty well given up anything that could be associated with the whites. (Colorado Historical Society)

could have taught the Czar and kings of the East much to their interest and to the happiness of their subjects. He was a model in habits, for he never chewed tobacco, abhorred whiskey, took but a sip of wine in company when it was offered, and then only as a matter of courtesy to his friends. He never swore nor used obscene or vulgar language. He was a firm believer in the Christian religion ... and united with the Methodist Church.

In the summer of 1876, bad fortune struck. Ouray visited a Canon City doctor and learned he had chronic nephritis (a kidney disease). His health began to go downhill, and he often felt fatigued. His back ached and his feet were often swollen. Dr. John H. Lacey was assigned to the agency and was constantly treating him. And accompanying the physical decline was a mental letdown. Ouray became depressed at the turn of events for the Utes. He was under constant tension and pressure from both the whites and the Utes. It was reported that he slept in a room with a Mexican and an Indian guard lying just outside the door.

Although the Tabeguache band remained faithful, Ouray began to have trouble controlling the other bands. The groups that gave Ouray the most trouble were the White River Utes under Captain Jack and Chief Douglas and the Southern Utes in the Southwest operating under Ignacio. White surveyors had again begun entering the Ute reservation and in some cases the Utes had attacked them. The Northern Utes were also upset that one of their members had not been made head chief by the government. Colorow fiercely opposed Ouray. But Ouray's strength and quickness to kill were well known and helped to keep the other Utes in line. For example, in the autumn of 1874, one of Ouray's men wished to build a fire and started to cut some wood within the enclosures of a white settler. Ouray ordered him back and told him that he must not trespass upon the property of the white man. The obstinate Ute replied that he would cut it anyway. Ouray answered that if he did, he would kill him. Both started for their guns, but Ouray was quicker and promptly shot him dead.

On another occasion, Ouray shot and broke the arm of the Indian Johnson, who afterward caused much of the trouble at the White River agency. Johnson had stolen some horses from white men and refused to return them when commanded to do so. In Ouray's eyes, he had brought disgrace upon the Ute Nation, for which he was punished.

The story of Hot Stuff is another example of an assassination attempt against Ouray. Wilson Rockwell, in **The Utes - A Forgotten People**, gives an account of the incident:

> Many of the Southern Utes felt for a time the same resentment and envy toward Ouray. One of these had been a student at the Carlisle Indian School. He

acquired the name of Hot Stuff at school because of an explosive accident which he had in his chemistry class. When Hot Stuff got out of the hospital, he went back to the reservation to live the life of a wild Indian.

He was bitter toward the whites and hated Ouray for being so cooperative and friendly with them. One day Ouray was informed by his secret police that Hot Stuff was on his way to the Uncompahgre Agency to kill him.

Late on the afternoon of the following day Chipeta happened to see Hot Stuff riding toward Ouray's home on a calico horse. The rider was approaching through a heavy growth of brush so as not to be seen. Chipeta pointed him out to her husband, who got his rifle. When Hot Stuff got within shooting range of the chief's adobe house, Ouray drew a bead on his enemy and shot him through the neck.

But mostly, agency life was quiet and uneventful. One diversion from the daily routine occurred in the fall of 1876 when the Uncompahgre agency became the central headquarters for mail going in and out to the nearby San Juan mines. Otto Mears coordinated the various mail-carrying contractors and divided the seventy-five-mile route from the agency to the Lake City road into three sections, with a cabin located every twenty-five miles. Mears also got the contract to carry food and supplies to the new agency. George Beckwith was picked by Mears to carry the mail by saddle horse and pack mule from the Uncompahgre agency to the Cimarron agency in New Mexico Territory. A week before the Christmas of 1876, Beckwith's pack mule went lame, so he rode out in search of one of the agency's mules or horses. He roped a mustang and tied the end of his lariat rope to his saddle horn. Something frightened the horse he was riding; Beckwith was thrown, and his rope tangled both horses. In struggling, the horses kicked and trampled Beckwith, who died a few days later and became the first white man buried in the area.

This photograph shows a very youthful-looking Chipeta; however, her clothing is identical with the attire that she is wearing in other pictures taken in Washington in 1880. The subjects of most portraits made during that time almost always bore a very stern countenance, but Chipeta is wearing her "Mona Lisa" smile in this picture. She was very beautiful, even in her old age, earning her the title of "Queen of the Utes," even though she was actually a Kiowa Apache. She could sing and play the guitar beautifully, but could also ride and hunt with the best of the white men. Perhaps the extreme compliment paid her, however, was that Chipeta was treated as a complete equal by Ouray at a time when women's rights had a long way to go. (Colorado Historical Society)

Trouble also came to the agency in other forms. Many claimed Ouray and certain white officials were misappropriating Ute money, and other smear campaigns were started by both the whites and the Utes against Ouray. Perhaps there was some truth to them. For example, Ouray received his salary on time but the federal

Agency employees and some of the local Utes posed for this photograph in front of the post office at the second Los Pinos agency on the Uncompahgre River near present day Colona. This building was made of adobe bricks, as were most of the buildings at the agency. For a time, mail to the town of Ouray and the surrounding mining districts was forwarded from this post office. Otto Mears contracted to get the mail from Saguache to the agency, and from there it was transported by another carrier under contract to Mears. Mears even asked for permission to build a toll road by way of the agency. Joseph B. Abbott, the agent, is the sixth from the right, and Moreno, the interpreter, is the third from the left. (Colorado Historical Society)

government often failed entirely to make the $25,000 annual tribal payments called for in the 1873 treaty.

In 1877, the Southern Ute agency was established at Ignacio, southwest of present day Durango, to serve the Mouache, Capote, and Weeminuche Utes. The Brunot Treaty of 1873 had stated that any of the Mouache or Capote Utes who were not already located on the Ute reservation in Colorado were to be moved there, but the agency had been located so far north of the Southern Utes that they had refused to travel there for their rations. Instead, they remained in New Mexico. As early as 1875, Alexander G. Irvine, the agent at Cimarron, New Mexico Territory, had reported to the U.S. government that about 350 Mouache Utes were located at the agency and asked that an attempt be made to have them moved. S.A. Russell, the other agent at Abiquiu, New Mexico Territory agreed with Irvine. He felt his Utes should also be moved from northern New Mexico to southwestern Colorado.

Two years elapsed before Congress acted on the requests of the agents. The Cimarron agency was ordered closed in 1876, but the Utes refused to leave the area until they had a new agency. In May, 1877, a permanent site for the new agency was selected on the Rio de los Pinos (the Pine River), where the original Los Pinos agency was supposed to have been built. But, by the end of the year, the agency had not been built, nor had the Indians been removed. In July of 1878, further legislation passed Congress, and the Utes at both Cimarron and Abiquiu were readied for their removal. By August 16, 1878, they had all been moved to the site of the new agency at Ignacio. Henry Page was the first agent. He and Edgar G. Bates built the first log cabin on the spot. It was the culmination of twenty years of effort to get the Utes out of New Mexico Territory.

In 1878, George Hurlburt began work at the Uncompahgre agency and helped lay out the first irrigation system. He also tended the fields since the Ute women spent much of their time away from the agency herding their goats. In addition, he helped man the agency store and reported that the Indians were honest and enjoyed playing practical jokes. He further noted that they loved the area for winter camping, but he couldn't understand why the Utes would pitch their tents in the cedars about a mile from the river so that the squaws were forced to carry water long distances. As to Ouray, he reported:

> Chief Ouray was a very dignified person, sedate, usually very quiet and spoke but little. He, as well as most of the men folk of the Indians, spoke but little English, using a sort of mongrel Spanish, totally devoid of grammatical order. Chief Ouray and his wife, Chipeta, were the only Indians who ever sat at the table with the agent and employees around the Agency. They were always welcome and were frequently guests at dinnertime ... I will add that Chief Ouray was a great friend of the whites, always urging the Indians to be at peace with them.

Ouray's health continued to decline, however. He was now reported to be suffering from both rheumatism and nephritis and was increasingly in pain. It became obvious to his white friends that he was not at all well.

In 1878, Ft. Lewis was established at Pagosa Springs, Colorado, to control the Southern Utes, then later was moved to a site near present day Durango. The Indian Bureau realized that the long, narrow strip of reservation in southwestern Colorado was very unworkable. The Southern Ute agent reported in 1878 that the cattle from the ranches on both sides kept coming onto the reservation. Finally, Congress passed a law on May 3, 1879, authorizing the President to enter into negotiations to try to move all the Utes to one agency. General Hatch, Lot M. Morrill, and N.C. McFarland were appointed as commissioners. The commission was to also try to get the Utes to give up the southern part of their reservation. They did eventually negotiate a change, but before it could be approved by Congress, the Meeker Massacre occurred, causing an entirely different result.

More and more, the whites were calling for the Utes to be removed entirely from Colorado. The settlers in the San Juans wished to spread into the valleys occupied by the Utes in order to farm and ranch. A prime example was the Uncompahgre Valley. It had been specifically reserved for the Utes from that land ceded in 1873 because of the Ute ancestral hot springs there. The Utes used the springs to cure many of their illnesses. But the area around the hot springs was the only area of tillable land for dozens of miles into the San Juans. In 1876, the farmers and ranchers began to move into the valley. Ouray protested to Agent Wheeler, who merely advised Ouray not to worry, that the land was in fact the Utes'. He said he would remove the trespassers, but nothing ever happened. General Edward Hatch appeared shortly thereafter and argued for days, trying to get the Utes either to move to the Oklahoma Indian Territory, to sell the southern part of their reservation and move to the north, or, at the very least, to give up the territory now occupied by the whites. An agreement to move out of the fertile upper Uncompahgre Valley was the only result. On August 17, 1876, the President signed an executive order by which the sacred springs and adjoining land in the Uncompahgre Valley (also known as the four-mile strip) were recognized as being Ute territory although they were to lose it only a few years later.

Another example of the whites' attempt to move into the valleys occurred in the spring of 1879 when gold was discovered at what later was the townsite of Dallas, about five miles into the reservation and ten miles south of the Los Pinos II agency. A city of tents sprung up overnight. Ouray was immediately aware that the prospectors were there but allowed them to stay. He said he didn't think they would find gold, but if they did, they could stay only as long as they built no houses. By the end of the summer, it was evident that Ouray was right. No appreciable gold had been found and the miners left.

Colorado had become a state in 1876, and many citizens of the area felt that the Indians were discouraging additional settlers. When Governor Frederick W. Pitkin took over the helm of government, he addressed the Colorado legislature, stating:

> Along the western borders of the State, and on the Pacific Slope, lies a vast tract occupied by the tribe of Ute Indians, as their reservation. It contains about twelve million acres and is nearly three times as large as the State of Massachusetts. It is watered by large stream and rivers, and contains many rich valleys and a large number of fertile plains. The climate is milder than in most localities of the same altitude on the Atlantic slope. Grasses grow there in great

In this picture, Ouray is standing next to Ignacio, chief of the Weeminuche band of Southern Utes. It has been said that Ouray liked to affect white man's ways and style of dress, yet in most of the photographs taken of him, he is in Indian garb, whereas the other Indians depicted are usually dressed as Ignacio is in this picture. Ignacio, who was six feet, two inches tall, was one of the tallest of the Utes; in comparison, Ouray was only five feet, seven inches. Ignacio was five years older than Ouray but outlived him by many, many years. The son of a medicine man, Ignacio had firm control over his band. (Denver Public Library)

luxuriance, and nearly every kind of grain and vegetables can be raised without difficulty.

This tract contains nearly one-third of the arable land of Colorado, and no portion of the State is better adapted for agricultural and grazing purposes than many portions of this reservation. Within its limits are large mountains, from most of which explorers have been excluded by Indians. Prospectors, however, have explored some portions of the country, and found valuable lode and placer claims, and there is reason to believe that it contains great mineral wealth.

The number of Indians who occupy this reservation is about three thousand. If the land was divided up between individual members of the tribe, it would give every man, woman, and child a homestead of between three and four thousand acres. It has been claimed that the entire tribe have had in cultivation about fifty acres of land, and from some personal knowledge of the subject I believe that one able-bodied white settler would cultivate more land than the whole tribe of Utes. These Indians are fed by the government, are allowed ponies without number, and except when engaged in an occasional hunt, their most serious employment is horse-racing. If this reservation could be extinguished, and the land thrown open to settlers, it will furnish homes to thousands of people of the state who desire homes.

Governor Pitkin's secretary, and former newspaperman William B. Vickers, who conducted an anti-Ute campaign in his **Denver Republican**, also got into the act. He wrote many, many anti-Ute pieces for **The Denver Tribune**, including the following:

Though not particularly quarrelsome or dangerous, the Utes are exceedingly disagreeable neighbors. Even if they would be content to live on their princely reservation, it would not be so bad, but they have a disgusting habit of ranging all over the state, stealing horses, killing off game, and carelessly firing forests in the dry summer season.

The Government should be shamed to foster and encourage these Utes in their idleness and wanton waste of property. Living off the bounty of a paternal but idiotic Indian Bureau, they actually become too lazy to draw their rations in the regular way, but insist on taking what they want wherever they find it. But for the fact that they are arrant cowards, as well as arrant knaves, the Western Slope of Colorado would be untenanted by the white race. Almost every year

The original Fort Lewis at Pagosa Springs was moved to a site on the La Plata River in 1881 when it was feared that the Utes might cause trouble because of the white man's efforts to get them out of Colorado. The military garrison was withdrawn in 1891, and the old fort became a boarding school for Indians and then a high school. Because the fort was on Indian land when the State of Colorado appropriated it for an agricultural college, the Indians were given free tuition. Later, that school was moved to Durango and became a four-year college, but the free tuition agreement still remains in effect. (Colorado Historical Society)

they threaten some of the white settlers with certain death if they do not leave the country, and, in some instances, they have tried to drive off white citizens, but the latter pay little attention to their vaporings ...

Philanthropists down East and abroad may mourn over the decadence of this once powerful tribe of Indians, but even a philanthropist would fail to find any occasion for regret if he came to Colorado and

Guero was a war chief of the Utes and was closely associated with Ouray. Some people have confused him with Guera Murah, Ouray's father. But considering when the photographs of Guero were taken, this seems impossible, for he looks only a few years older than Ouray in the picture. There are also references to Guera Murah and Guero being at the same place at the same time. Finally, it seems strange that none of the contemporaries of the time pointed Guero out as Ouray's father when they were constantly referring to any relationship, no matter how remote, that Ouray or Chipeta had with the Other Utes of their time. (Denver Public Library)

made a study of Ute character and habits. Though better in some high (and low) respects than the Digger Indians of Arizona, or the Paiutes of Nevada, the Colorado Utes have nothing in common with the Indians of history and romance, whose "wrongs" have been so tearfully portrayed by half-baked authors. The strongest prejudices of Eastern people in favor of the Indians give way before the strong disgust inspired by closer acquaintance.

Henry M. Teller was elected one of Colorado's first two senators, and he was also violently anti-Indian. Teller, Vickers, and many of Colorado's citizens wanted the Utes removed. They were opposed by Carl Schurz, Secretary of the Interior, who thought the Utes should stay where they were, but should accept land allotments and live like the white man. The anti-Indian groups began to look for some excuse to force the Utes to move, and it soon came in the form of the Meeker Massacre.

Chapter Nine

THE BATTLE OF MILK CREEK— THE MEEKER MASSACRE

The final outburst of Ute frustration occurred in 1879 among the White River Utes. In part, it was undoubtedly encouraged by the whites, who were looking for an excuse to get the stubbornly friendly Utes out of Colorado.

The United States had been negotiating with the Mouache, Capote, and Weeminuche Utes for consolidation of their lands into a single agency, which culminated in an agreement reached at Pagosa Springs on November 9, 1878. Those Utes released their rights to, and interests in, that part of the Confederated Ute Reservation lying south of 38° 10' North latitude. The new agency was to be in the White River area, and twenty thousand dollars was allocated for construction of the agency itself.

Nathan Meeker was to be the second agent at the new agency. Meeker, principal founder of the town of Greeley, was nearly sixty-one years of age when he was sent to White River. He brought with him his wife and his seventeen-year-old daughter, Josephine, who was to be the agency school teacher. Meeker was deeply in debt and saw the appointment as a way to get out of financial trouble. Although a man of ideals and a competent organizer, he did not have even the simplest understanding of the Utes. He was an uncompromising man—naive and self-righteous—and was determined to do good and turn the Utes into progressive, self-sustaining farmers, whether it was by education or by force. Many of those who encouraged him felt that such an attempt would cause an incident that would lead to the Utes' removal from Colorado.

Sixty-year-old Douglas was technically the chief of the White River Utes, but he was losing followers to the much younger sub-chiefs. Captain Jack and Johnson never recognized Douglas as their chief, nor did they get along with Ouray. Captain Jack was a ferocious warrior, and Johnson was the group's medicine man and a deadly shot. Each of the three, however, had about an equal number of loyal followers. The stage was set for trouble.

When Meeker arrived at the agency on May 10, 1878, he found that conditions were bad. His predecessor at the agency had instituted an agricultural program, but it was looked upon as despicable and insulting work by the Utes. The Indians had almost starved to death the previous winter. Many of them left the reservation in order to hunt, and to make matters worse, even the whites

Nathan C. Meeker was the agent at the White River agency at the time of the Ute uprising on September 29, 1879. "Father Meeker," as he wanted the Indians to call him, was a sincere but unwise agent who believed he could Christianize, civilize, and change the nomadic Ute hunter into a farmer. He provoked the massacre by plowing up Ute Johnson's pony pasture and race track as a punitive act to teach the Indian who was boss. He believed that the Indian had the mental development of a small child, but failed to conceal that feeling from the Utes themselves, which was probably his greatest error. He couldn't understand why the Utes wouldn't want to become just like himself. (Denver Public Library)

Although the Indians evidently considered leaving her behind, Mrs. Arvilla Smith Meeker, wife of the agent, was kidnapped and taken to a temporary mountain camp at the time of the attack on the Meeker agency. She was subjected to many indignities and, being elderly, suffered a psychological trauma from which she never fully recovered. Her descriptions of her experiences were therefore somewhat unreliable: it was never certain how much of her story was true and how much the result of hysteria. She did have kind words for Chipeta, who made the hostages welcome in her home after they had been rescued and brought to Chief Ouray's camp. (Denver Public Library)

in the area were having hard times. Some of them were coming onto the reservation and killing much of what little Indian game was left. Meeker thought the Indians were lazy—all they did was hunt and race their ponies, and they only dug their one irrigation ditch after a threatened loss of annuities. What he failed to realize was that for centuries, Ute culture had been built around allowing the male Ute to be able to do anything that he felt free to do, as long as he provided for his family.

In the summer of 1879, hundreds of forests fires were breaking out all over Colorado, and rumors began to spread that the Utes were responsible. Evidently, it was presumed that they were trying to burn the white man out from around the edge of the reservation. In fact, it was the Utes who depended heavily on the forests for their game, and it was later proved that most of the fires were started by careless white men. William Vickers (who many said was spreading the rumors) wrote and obtained permission from the Indian Bureau to use military force if necessary to keep the Utes on the reservation. Vickers also wrote several newspaper articles suggesting that the Utes were extremely lazy—even accusing them of being too lazy to go pick up their rations. The Utes, in fact, were unhappy because they had not been receiving their food and supplies, which were being held for storage costs in a railroad warehouse. Many of their cattle were also being lost to whites; in early 1879, it was reported that over twelve hundred head had already been stolen.

Although the United States was pressuring the Utes to become farmers and ranchers, little progress was being made. The Utes had some small herds, mainly sheep, and some of the women had small gardens. But hunting was still the basis of their economy: the men hunted and the women tanned the hides and made clothes for their families. Meeker wasn't having any better luck than any other white man in convincing the Utes that they should start farming. A small group of Utes even paid a call on Governor Pitkin to ask him to help stop Meeker's fence-building and plowing. They had lost all respect for Meeker and wanted another agent. The anti-Indian governor did nothing.

The immediate cause of the White River uprising happened in September of 1879, about a year after Meeker's arrival at the agency, when he plowed up part of the Ute horse racing track, supposedly to prepare the land for planting crops. It is more likely that he was mad at Johnson for using grain for his racehorses that had been allocated for the work horses. The Utes considered the plowing of the ground itself as a desecration of the earth. In addition to destroying their race track, the Utes resented the white man's attempt to force them to do what they considered woman's work. They naturally wanted to keep their carefree ways. Johnson (the husband of Ouray's sister Susan) stopped the plowing by firing shots at the team trying to break the ground.

On September 10, Meeker cornered Johnson and threatened to make him kill most of his ponies. Johnson reacted by throwing

Meeker against a hitching post, and they had a short fist fight. Meeker was more hurt mentally than physically, but sent for troops from Ft. Steele, Wyoming. The same day he wrote the following letter:

White River Agency, Colo.
September 10, 1879

Hon. E. A. Hoyt
Commissioner, Washington, D.C.

I have been assaulted by a leading Chief, Johnson, forced out of my own house, and injured badly, but was rescued by employees. It is now revealed that Johnson originated all the trouble stated in letter September 8th. His son shot at the plowman, and the opposition to plowing is wide. Plowing stops. Life of self, family, and employees not safe; want protection immediately; have asked Governor Pitkin to confer with General Pope.

N.C. Meeker
Indian Agent

The Utes were adamant that soldiers were not to come onto Ute land; however, Major T.T. Thornburgh left from Ft. Steele, Wyoming, on September 22 with thirty-three supply wagons, three companies of cavalry, and one company of infantry (a total of 178 men). On September 26, Thornburgh's command was met by Captain Jack, Colorow, Sowerwich, and two other Utes, who told him that all was in order at the agency and that soldiers didn't need to come onto the reservation. Thornburgh replied that the soldiers were only going to the agency to investigate rumors of trouble.

When they were about forty-five miles away from the White River agency, Thornburgh and his troops were approached by Wilmer Eskridge (an emissary from the Meeker agency), Captain Jack, and Colorow. Eskridge delivered a message from Meeker and the Utes at the agency requesting a peace council before the soldiers came any closer. It was suggested that only Thornburgh and five soldiers go to the agency. Chief Colorow stated that he was authorized to guarantee Thornburgh's safety at the agency, and recommended that the soldiers stay at a grassy spot on Deer Creek, about fifty miles from the Agency.

On September 29, Thornburgh disregarded the advice. Colorow and Jack warned him that the Indians would fight if his troops crossed Milk Creek onto the Ute reservation. They were afraid that, with so many men, the soldiers might indeed arrest and punish them as Meeker kept threatening. Although it had been fifteen years since the Sand Creek Massacre, the Indians were still worried that such a massacre could occur again. Thornburgh evidently thought there would not be a fight and continued to advance across

Major Thomas T. Thornburgh, upon receiving orders to aid agent Meeker, marched about 120 miles with two hundred men from Ft. Steele, near Rawlins, Wyoming. When Thornburgh crossed Milk Creek with the troops (which he promised the Utes he wouldn't do), the Indians were already in place, ready to stage an ambush. Major Thornburgh should have marched to the left or right side of the little valley, but took the easier route up the center. It was a deadly trap since it gave the Indians the strategic advantage and the protection of the rocks and the crest of the hill. In the first few minutes of fighting, Thornburgh and all of his officers above the rank of captain had been killed. (Denver Public Library)

the reservation line. He sent a letter to Meeker, which read in part:

> I have carefully considered whether or not it would be advisable to have my command at a point as distant as that desired by the Indians, and have reached the conclusion that under my orders, which require me to march my command to the agency, I am not at liberty to leave it at a point where it would not be available in case of trouble.

The soldiers continued their march. Then, as they were passing through Red Canyon, some twenty-five miles north of the agency, about one hundred Utes attacked. Many of the Indians were armed

only with bows and arrows, but a large number also had rifles. They hid behind the boulders and along the ridges. Which side fired the first shot is not known for sure, but a terrific volley of bullets and arrows from the Utes stopped Thornburgh's advance. Nine men were killed immediately. When Thornburgh tried to make a quick charge to his supply wagons, he was caught in a deadly crossfire and was killed. The troops were forced to dig in and defend themselves as best they could, having to sacrifice their horses and mules to use them for protection. The Utes burned the brush around the soldiers so that they were entirely exposed and cut off from water. During the first night of the siege, a scout, Joe Rankin, escaped and rode 160 miles in twenty-eight hours to get reinforcements in Wyoming.

The Utes were to keep the army pinned down for almost a week. Eventually, thirteen soldiers were killed and forty-three were wounded. The Utes later reported that thirty-seven of their men had been killed, including Wattseonavot, Chief Ouray's nephew.

A few hours after Thornburgh was attacked, Chief Douglas and about twenty other Utes killed Meeker and eight other white men on the agency grounds. Three other white men were killed nearby. The three women and two children who were at the agency were taken hostage by Douglas and were eventually held for twenty-three days. Most of the agency buildings were pillaged and burned.

Captain Payne and forty-three men of the black Ninth Cavalry (also called the Buffalo soldiers) arrived the third day of the siege, but there still weren't enough men to rout the Indians. Colonel Wesley Merritt and his command of 550 men from Wyoming arrived on the sixth day of the siege. Their advance had hardly begun when a runner with a white flag appeared among the Indians. He was Joseph Brady, a miller at Los Pinos. Accompanying him was a Ute sent by Chief Ouray, who had ordered the Indians to stop fighting. As the firing ceased, the Indians scattered and fled. Ouray had heard of the uprising the same day that Scout Rankin reached help in Wyoming, and had initially responded with mixed emotions. On the one hand, he experienced a justifiable urge

The memorial to Major Thornburgh and his soldiers who were killed or wounded sits in the middle of the flat valley in which the battle took place. To its credit, the federal government did consider Milk Creek to be a military engagement in which its forces had been defeated and did not demand the surrender of the Ute leaders in the battle. However, it did decide that the events at the agency were a massacre and demanded that the Indians who participated be delivered for trial and punishment. The governor of Colorado went even further and said that if the Indians didn't abandon their land or the government move them, the Utes should simply be exterminated. (Denver Public Library)

The White River (Meeker) Massacre and the Battle of Milk Creek were widely publicized all over the United States. These sketches from "Harper's Weekly Magazine" depict part of the scenes at the agency at the time of the massacre. At the top is a sketch of Johnson's cabin. The bottom scene occurred when Frank Dresser, one of the agency employees, came to the inner room of a building where the women were hiding. Josephine Meeker picked up a gun from off the bed and said, "Here, Frank, this is Mr. Price's gun." He fired twice from a window and helped the women slip into the milk house, which offered a little more security for a time. (Colorado Historical Society)

to join his people and retaliate against the whites because the government troops had no right to be on the Indian land and his people had definitely been provoked into rebelling. But Ouray also realized that the actions of the Meeker Indians had sealed the fate of all Utes: they would have to be moved.

It is said that Ouray and Chipeta talked late into the night. Although Chipeta is said to have ridden for a day to find Ouray, who was out hunting when the news of the massacre came in, it is likely that she only sent a runner. Chipeta is also supposed to have pleaded and cried tears for peace. In any event, Ouray decided not to join Douglas, and Chief Ignacio made it clear the Southern Utes would not participate either. Ouray sent the runner to ask the White River Utes to back out of the situation. Ouray's sister Susan was also said to have helped persuade the rebellious Utes to lay down their arms.

The Utes sullenly agreed to Ouray's request; however, it will never be known if it was actually Ouray's order that caused the Utes to back off or if it was the fact that the militant fifty or sixty Utes were now facing almost one thousand U.S. troops. When it was clear what Ouray was trying to do, the army quickly pulled General Merritt and his relief forces out of the situation.

After the fighting stopped, the army troops were told to stay put while Utes and white men from Los Pinos agency began negotiations to try to recover the white women at Meeker. The Indians had left the agency and were running with the women, warning that they would kill them if the soldiers came too close. Interior Secretary Carl Schurz appointed Charles Adams, a special agent, to gain the women's release. He proceeded from Denver to Chief Ouray's camp for advice and help, then left on October 19, accompanied by Sapovanero, Shavano, Colorow, twelve other Utes, George Sherman (the clerk of the agency), Captain M.W. Cline, William Saunders (a local newspaperman), and for some unknown reason, Count Doenhoff from the Austrian embassy. Ouray is supposed to have sent along his own tent for the use of the women.

THE HOUSE OF JOHNSON, SUB-CHIEF OF THE UTES ON THE AGENCY FARM.

Ouray had said that Douglas could probably be found somewhere on Plateau Creek between the present towns of Palisade and DeBeque. The relief group went totally unarmed. Adams carried only orders from Ouray for immediate cessation of any hostilities and for the surrender of the captives. They found Douglas's camp at Grand Mesa on October 21, but Douglas refused to release the women until he had some assurances that the relief column of soldiers following him had been stopped. A four-hour conference followed, during which Adams assured Douglas the column would not stop until the women were released, and Susan evidently made an impassioned plea for the captives' release. Sapovanero finally helped break the stalemate by telling Douglas that Ouray had said that if the women weren't released immediately and delivered to Ouray's farm by October 24, then all of the other Ute bands would come after them. Douglas agreed to give the women up.

Miss Josephine Meeker gave this account of the order:
> Next morning we left for Uncompahgre ... to Chief Ouray's house on the Uncompahgre River near Los Pinos. We rode on ponies forty miles the first three days and reached Captain Cline's wagons on a small

This sketch in "Frank Leslie's Illustrated Newspaper" of December 6, 1879, depicts the scene at the agency when the soldiers arrived days later. Two graves, complete with head and foot markers, suggest that the bodies were buried right where they were found. The one on the left is that of N.C. Meeker; the one on the right bears the name of W.H. Post. The building still standing is probably the milk house, where the women and children hid until smoke, coming in from one small window, caused them to abandon their sanctuary and attempt to escape into the sagebrush. The milk house was double-walled, with adobe in between to make it cooler; this type of structure was also more fire resistant. (Denver Public Library)

tributary of the Grand. Here we took the buck-board wagon and travelled next day to the Gunnison River and the next and last day of fear we travelled forty-five miles and reached the house of good Chief Ouray about sundown.

Here Inspector Pollock and my brother Ralph met me, and I was happy enough. Chief Ouray and his noble wife did everything possible to make us comfortable. We found carpets on the floor and curtains on the windows, lamps on the tables and stoves in the rooms, with fires burning. We were given a whole house, and after supper we went to bed without much fear, though mother was haunted by the terrors she had passed through. Next morning we breakfasted with Mrs. Ouray who shed tears over us as she bade us goodbye ...

Flora Pice, one of the other women who had been at the Meeker agency, added that Ouray spoke broken English, but that he conversed in eloquent and melodious Spanish, and that his words were always delivered with great fluency:

We were well treated at Ouray's house. It had Brussels carpets, window curtains, stoves, good beds, glass windows, spittoons, rocking chairs, camp stools, mirrors and an elegantly carved bureau. We were received as old and long lost friends. Mrs. Ouray wept for our hardships and her motherly face, dusky but beautiful with sweetness and compassion, was wet with tears. We left her crying ...

During the Meeker Massacre, Governor Pitkin did nothing to help keep the Utes and whites calm, and, in fact, started near panic among the whites when he sent a telegraph message throughout the state that read: "Indians off their reservation, seeking to destroy your settlements by fire, are game to be hunted and destroyed like wild beasts ... General Hatch rushing regulars to the San Juan." Furthermore, Pitkin created three military districts, one to cover each of the major bands of Utes. Rumors flew that the Indians were killing and burning everywhere and that Ouray had said he couldn't control his people. None of this, of course, was true. As a matter of fact, agent Stanley felt compelled to write to Commissioner Hoyt on October 15:

I hope and trust the Indian Department at Washington will use every influence to see that the Utes have a fair hearing in this matter, that the world may know who is to blame, the Utes or the white cormorants surrounding them. I am absolutely disgusted at the conduct of the white people and am not at all surprised that the Indians do occasionally turn upon the traducers and robbers of their rights. The worm will

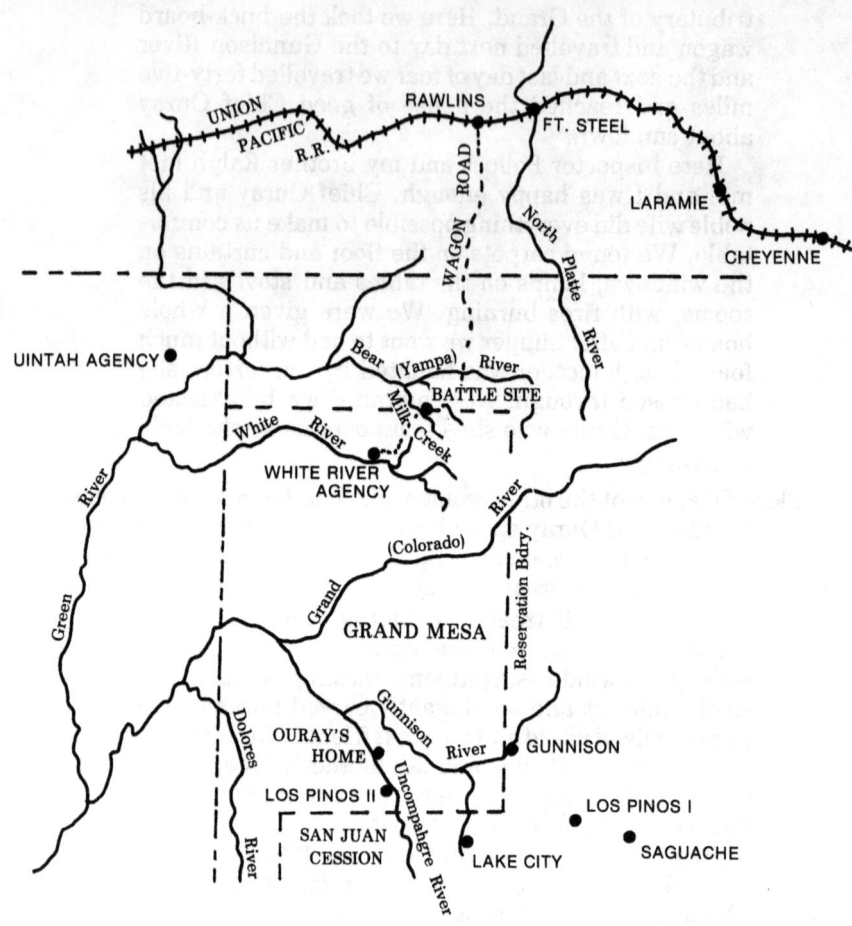

NORTHERN UTE RESERVATION 1879

When Meeker called for help at the White River agency, Major T.T. Thornburgh left Ft. Steele, Wyoming, and headed south along the wagon road. He was met at the reservation line near Milk Creek. Thornburgh originally agreed to station his troops here, taking just four or five men with him to see if Meeker was okay. But he changed his mind, deciding he should move his troops closer. When he crossed Milk Creek, the Indians attacked. A few hours later, the Meeker Massacre occurred. Ouray, who was not party to the incident, sent a messenger, who arrived six days into the Milk Creek siege, and was able to get the Indians to lay down their arms. In the meanwhile, Douglas had fled with the white women to the Grand Mesa area, where they were later found and taken to Ouray's home.

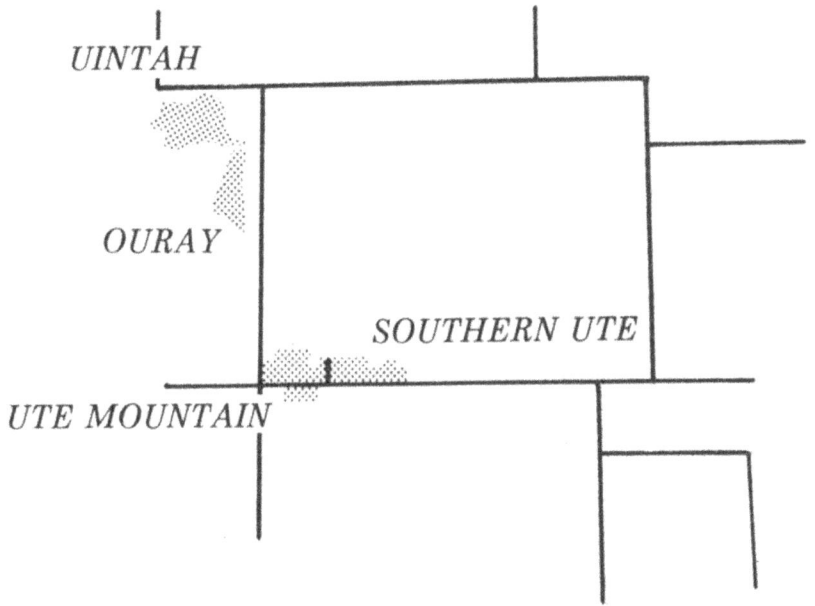

PRESENT UTE TERRITORY

After the Meeker Massacre, several small reservations were created for the Utes in southwestern Colorado and northeastern Utah. The White River and Tabeguache Utes went to a reservation in Utah that was later named after Chief Ouray. Originally, they and the Uintahs had much more land than indicated on this map, but the whites took much of that away too. (A recent court decision indicates that they may get that land back.) Later, the Ute Mountain and the Southern Ute reservations were created out of what had originally been one agency. When Mesa Verde became a national park, a part of the Ute Mountain land, now in the park, was traded for additional federal lands.

squirm when tread upon and the noble horse defend himself when goaded to desperation, and why not an Indian, one of God's people, who is covered by the same divine mantle of charity that enrobes the whites, and are as devout worshippers in their simple way at the seat of justice and mercy as the white man, with none of the white man's hypocrisy and studied cant.

However, the agent's sentiments were not echoed by everyone. **The Ouray Times** of October 25, 1879, under a headline of "The Utes Must Go," stated that "this is the most popular text in Colorado, and notwithstanding the objections thereto of H. Stanley and the rest of the Indian lovers."

But the scare wore off quickly as it became obvious that the Tabeguache and Southern Utes weren't going to join the uprising.

About this time, Ouray suffered a personal tragedy: his uncle and nephew were killed by soldiers. Ouray said the incident occurred before the Meeker uprising, but the whites said it happened a short time afterwards. The soldiers said they had shot them because they had guns. Chief Ouray pointed out that the Utes were hunting beaver, and the fact that his kin could be killed without provocation struck Ouray deeply. He referred to this incident many times in the coming months.

Following the Meeker Massacre, the United States appointed a commission headed by General Edward Hatch to investigate the incident and bring the guilty Utes to trial. The commission met at the Uncompahgre agency from November 12 to January 7, 1880, trying to find out exactly who had committed the murders. Ouray was irked because the interpreter was translating with a decided slant against the Utes. He believed that he or several other Utes could have been doing a better job. On November 16, Ouray told the commission:

> I do not want to be a chief. I grow old and am tottering. Let some young man with the fire of youth in his veins take my place. I have my farm which I would rather cultivate and watch the seed planted by me grow up to maturity than to be head chief. They all

> **Miss Josephine Meeker, daughter of the agent at White River, also had a function in "civilizing" the Indians, for she was the school teacher for those who had any desire to learn how to read or write. Her description of her life in captivity indicates that she was subjected to unspeakable indignities. For quite a while after she was rescued and returned to civilization, she traveled about, giving lectures on her experiences and her knowledge of the Indians, which served to keep the anti-Indian sentiment alive until all of the Utes could be removed from the State of Colorado. (Denver Public Library)**

come to me with their troubles. I know everything and have all their burdens to bear. Washington no want me to give up my position, wants me to stay and govern Utes. I want only to be known as Ouray, the friend of the white man.

The Meeker Massacre and the Battle of Milk Creek were recreated dozens of times by various artists, including such notables as Frederick Remington. The artist of this painting is unknown, but he has provided a good example of the way in which liberties were taken with the facts. At the right, the white man appears to be leaving; he has a gun but seems to have no intention of using it. Tepees are clustered too closely around the cabins. In the center background, some Ute is going about his business, transporting something on a horse-drawn travois. At left are two Indians contesting over a white girl. Only in the center of the painting does it appear that someone might be getting killed. A nice piece of art, but the artist obviously never studied the scene of the massacre! (Colorado Historical Society)

On November 17, Ouray asked to make a statement and the following dialogue between Ouray and Hatch occurred:

    Chief Ouray: I cannot do more than I have at present. The Indians will not testify to any more. If you give me time, say two or three months, I can find out the guilty ones and punish them.

    General Hatch: If we grant you this time, will you accompany us, in the mean time, to Rawlins to hear the evidence of the officers and soldiers?

    Chief Ouray: No, I will go to Washington, but no where else.

    General Hatch: Do you mean you prefer to go to Washington to settle these difficulties?

    Chief Ouray: Yes, I want to take other chiefs and go to Washington to talk over this matter. I know the Indians will not say anything here, but believe they will speak the truth in Washington.

General Hatch: How many chiefs do you want to go to Washington?

Chief Ouray: I think eight of the principal chiefs will be enough.

Hatch wrote to Carl Schurz to see if up to ten Utes could be brought to Washington. He then continued to take testimony. Ouray missed several of the next days of the investigation because of illness or perhaps because he didn't want to attend. On November 20, word was received that the Utes could come to Washington, but Hatch kept taking testimony. Ouray took the position that the United States could not try the guilty parties. He even refused to help identify them. None of the Indians would talk. On December 7, a list of twelve suspects was finally drawn up by the women who had been held captive. Ouray objected to taking the testimony of women against men as being contrary to Ute custom, and said he thought the women had just given the name of every Ute they could remember. He stated that the White River Utes had all directly or indirectly been engaged in the massacre and that a man could not be compelled to testify against himself. Finally, General Hatch and Adams ordered Chief Ouray to have the twelve men named by the women brought in for trial or Hatch would move his army forward onto the Ute lands. The details of what happened next were given by a Ouray, Colorado newspaper, **The Solid Muldoon:**

> A death silence fell upon everything. Nothing was said and no one moved for a few minutes. Then Colorow lighted a long pipe and each Indian present drew his knife and laid it on his knee ... Each Indian present dropped his hand down to his waist and laid it upon his knife or revolver. Each white man did the same, and the two parties remained in this position, each urging the glittering gage of battle and each waiting an agressive movement on the part of the other ... Twenty-five Indians to six whites were terrible odds and the fifteen soldiers in the next room could not have gotten into the room in time to rescue the endangered commission. Finally Ouray spoke: "We cannot deliver up to you these Indians unless they are to be tried at Washington. They must not be tried in Colorado. The Colorado people are all our enemies, and to give our men up to be tried in this state would be as if we gave them up, knowing that they would be hung instantly.
>
> We will bring these men here for you to see, and those whom you decide to be guilty shall be taken to Washington, and the President shall determine their guilt or innocence. Douglas will have to go. None of us deny that he was engaged in the White River troubles,

Captain Jack, leader of the successful attack on Thornburgh, outsmarted and outmaneuvered his white cavalry adversary. Thornburgh told the Utes he would halt his command before going past Milk Creek and would go in with only four or five soldiers to talk with Meeker. He changed his mind and decided to move his troops closer in case something went wrong and they were needed. The Utes saw the move as an indication that he was going to attack them. They evidently suspected a double-cross or a surprise attack such as the one at Sand Creek, so they were prepared, and attacked when Thornburgh crossed the river. (Colorado Historical Society)

> and you shall decide who else is to go. Upon this condition and no others will we deliver these Indians ... You three (pointing to Hatch, Adams and Valois, the legal adviser) are all my enemies. I am one against three. You hate me. You are residents of Colorado and New Mexico and a French devil (alluding to Valois), I have not one friend among you. You will not give me justice, and that is why I want to go to Washington where I will, at least, have one friend."

The friend in Washington that Ouray alluded to was Secretary of the Interior Carl Schurz.

Ouray stated that the Utes would not leave—that they would fight, if necessary, for their land. He indicated he felt the Utes could hold out at least for awhile in the mountains. Ouray told William Saunders, correspondent for **The Ouray Times:**

> The Utes are not to blame in this. I told you when we were out hunting that I was having trouble in restraining my young men. White prospectors and hunters came on the reservation and shot the Utes when they saw them. You know yourselves that this happened. My uncle and my nephew were killed by the soldiers a few days ago, while they were hunting. The soldiers said that they had no right to have rifles. They have when they hunt.
>
> Meeker made the Utes work for his own glory and refused to feed them when they did not work as he wanted them to work. He had no right to do that. The Government in our treaty said nothing about work, but agreed to give us these lands and to give us supplies, blankets and food. They have violated that treaty and my men were angry. They heard that Meeker had sent for the soldiers to punish them for not working and coming to church, they always

remember what Chivington did to the Cheyennes, and they tried to prevent the soldiers from getting to the agency by killing them. Then they went crazy and killed Meeker and the other white men, and took the women and the children. They should not have done that.

From left to right in this picture are Chief Ignacio of the Southern Utes; Carl Schurz, Secretary of the Interior; Woretsiz; Ouray; General Charles Adams; and Chipeta. The photo was taken in Washington in 1880 during the treaty negotiations that would result in the removal of the White River and Tabeguache Utes to the Uintah Basin in present day Utah. This was to be the last of the trips Ouray made to Washington, D.C., since he died September 24 of that year. It is evident that he doesn't look as strong and healthy as in previous photographs. Chief Ignacio is seated on the chair that marks this as a Brady photo. (Colorado Historical Society)

Colorow and Jack were exonerated for taking part in the fight with Thornburgh. They were told that since they weren't at the agency, they wouldn't be punished. They undertook to bring in the twelve men whom the women swore had taken part in the massacre. At first, they could find only Douglas, but eventually they rounded up ten other Utes. However, none of the ten were on the list the Meeker women had made!

Otto Mears (who served as interpreter), Shavano, Jack, Sowerwich, Ouray, Chipeta, Ignacio, Buckskin Charlie, Severo, and Blanco left on January 16, 1880, to travel to Washington, D.C. Since the white men had made threats against the Utes, Adams took the precaution of having soldiers accompany the group.

Nevertheless, the Utes were verbally assaulted in Alamosa, and in Pueblo, two thousand whites screamed and yelled threats at the Utes. The soldiers guarded the Indians closely, but the crowd still kicked and pulled at them and threw rocks, sticks, and coal. Douglas accompanied the group only as far as Ft. Leavenworth, Kansas, where he was jailed but was released as insane 348 days later.

In Washington, Ouray and the rest of the Utes took part in a Congressional hearing on the Ute outbreak. For day after day, testimony was given by the whites while most of the Utes present could not even understand what was going on.

Before leaving, Ouray was examined by several Washington doctors, who all told him that he might only have a short time to live. He also visited with Secretary of the Interior Carl Schurz, who had immense respect for Ouray, and later said:

> In official conversation (Ouray's) talk was quite different from that of the ordinary Indian chief. He spoke like a man of a high order of intelligence and of larger views who had risen above the prejudices and aversions of his race, and expressed his thoughts in language clear and precise, entirely unburdened by the figures of speech and superfluities commonly current in Indian talk.
>
> He had evidently pondered much over the condition and future of the Indians of North America and expressed his mature conclusions with the simple eloquence of a statesman. He comprehended perfectly the utter hopelessness of the struggle of the Indians against the progress of civilization. He saw clearly that nothing was left to them but to accommodate themselves to civilized ways or perish. He admitted that it was very hard to make his people understand this; that so long as they did not fully appreciate it, they should, as much as possible, be kept out of harm's way; that it was the duty of influential chiefs to cooperate with the Government to make the transition as little dangerous and painful as possible; that he, therefore, recognized the necessity of removing the Utes from Colorado, hard as the parting from their old haunts might be, and that he depended on me to bring about that removal under conditions favorable to his people.
>
> Ouray was by far the brightest Indian I have ever met.

Later, after Ouray's death, Chipeta was to send a touching letter to Schurz along with a gift of the clothes that Ouray had worn when he was in Washington, D.C., his pouch, and his powder horn. She asked that they be accepted as a token of friendship.

The Utes were finally allowed to give their testimony before the Congressional committees. It had been agreed almost immediately after the Meeker Massacre that the White River Utes were to move. But the Uncompahgre and Southern Utes didn't like being asked to move again because of something that the White River Utes had done (although two Tabeguache Utes participated in the massacre and, in fact, took two of the women captive). They pointed out that they had even helped to stop the trouble; that the whites should not have sent troops onto Ute land; and that Meeker himself was partly to blame. But the whites were insistent. The Utes knew it was hopeless. They had to sign—this time there was no bargaining.

On March 6, 1880, with the hearing still going on, a treaty was signed that originally provided for the removal of all seven Ute bands. The Utes agreed to continue to try to find the guilty parties in the Meeker Massacre. The White River Utes were to go to the Uintah reservation in Utah. The Tabeguaches were to go to near present day Grand Junction at the junction of the Grand (Colorado) and Gunnison rivers. If enough agricultural land was not available there, then they were to go on into Utah. Although they were originally supposed to leave, the southern Utes were allowed to stay where they were in Southern Colorado. The Utes were to take their new land as individuals and not as tribes as a whole. The treaty would not become effective unless ratified by three-fourths of the Ute males.

Provision was made for allotments of 160 acres of agricultural land and additional grazing land not to exceed 160 acres for each head of a family. Allotments of eighty acres of agricultural land with additional grazing land of not more than eighty acres were also to be made for each single Ute over eighteen who was not the head of a family, to each orphan child under eighteen, and to each Ute then living and "not otherwise provided for."

The Department of the Interior estimated that there were three thousand heads of families and one thousand youths over eighteen who would be eligible for the allotments. The Utes were to receive, as a tribe, in addition to the annuities and benefits already provided for by the Treaty of 1873, enough money from the government to produce an income of $50,000 a year to be distributed per capita to them forever.

The treaty refused to pay anything to the White River Utes so long as any of the participants in the Meeker Massacre remained at large, and it stipulated that annual pension payments be made to dependents and victims of the massacre for twenty years from money that would otherwise go to the White River Utes. The land the Utes were vacating was to be sold to help pay the sums of money provided for in the treaty. The hearings in Washington ended on March 22 and the Utes left for Colorado.

Congress ratified the treaty on June 15, 1880, providing that three-fourths of the Utes had to sign it before October 15 of that year, or it would not become effective. A commission of five,

Standing at the rear of this photograph is William H. Berry, agent at the Uncompahgre agency, while in the front, from left to right, are Ojo Blanco (White Eye), Tapuch, Captain Jack, and Tim Johnson. Tim was imprisoned with Douglas at Leavenworth, but evidently cried so pitifully that the whites let him go on to Washington, D.C. Many of the Utes were well-traveled, perhaps more so than the average white at that time. Ouray went to Washington often enough that he was probably as familiar with that city as he was with the reservation. On every trip, part of the itinerary was to pose for official photographs. It is well for history that the Indians did this, for if they had not done so even many of the Ute names would not have survived. (Colorado Historical Society)

including Otto Mears of Colorado, was appointed by Congress to obtain the required number of Ute signatures. Ouray explained to his fellow Utes as best he could why they would have to leave their ancestral lands and why the agreement, as bad as it was, was the best they could hope for.

On July 21, 1880, a meeting was held at Los Pinos to get the individual Utes to sign the agreement; however, Ouray told the whites that he wasn't sure any of the Uncompahgre Utes would sign unless there were further negotiations. The agreement was not signed, and on July 28, 1880, another meeting was called. This time thirty-six Uncompahgre Utes and ten White River Utes signed. However, Chief Ouray was not one of them; he was now acutely ill with nephritis and even felt it necessary to appoint Sapovanero to act as temporary head chief. The whites then left for the Southern Ute agency to look for signatures. The Southern Utes were very reluctant. Virtually none of the individual Utes would ratify it, and it began to look like the treaty was doomed, especially in light of what was to come.

Chapter Ten

OURAY'S DEATH— THE UTES LEAVE COLORADO

On August 14, 1880, Ouray, Chipeta, her brother John McCook, and several other Utes left the Uncompahgre agency for the Southern Ute agency at Ignacio. Their purpose was probably to help induce the Southern Utes to sign the Treaty of 1880 and to meet with commissioners from Washington regarding payment of the Utes' money should the treaty be ratified. However, it is possible that Ouray was actually trying to stop Ignacio's group from signing. On the other hand, he knew he was very sick, and maybe he just wanted to visit his old friends before he died.

The band spent the night of August 16 about twelve miles north of Durango at Pinkerton Hot Springs and arrived at Ignacio on August 17, 1880. The commissioners were not present yet, and Ouray quietly made camp. Few even knew that he was there.

Will Burns, one of the local interpreters, learned of Ouray's presence by chance from one of the local Utes. He immediately went looking for Ouray's group and found their camp a few hundred yards north of the agency building on the west bank of the Pine River. When Burns entered Ouray's lodge, he discovered the old chief lying on blankets, only partly clothed in a breech-cloth, leggings, and moccasins. Burns could tell that something was the matter and was told by Ouray that he had not been feeling well since leaving the Uncompahgre agency. Burns asked if Ouray wanted a doctor, but received no answer. It was obvious that the situation was serious.

Burns went to the agency headquarters and reported what he had seen to the agent, Colonel Page. Page and the agency physician, Dr. E. F. Smith, immediately went to Ouray's tepee, where they found his stomach badly swollen. He was in quite a bit of pain and had a high fever. The doctor diagnosed Ouray's condition as an acute case of kidney trouble—probably Bright's Disease. He told the agent that Ouray was in very serious condition. Page sent a courier to Animas City (now a part of the City of Durango) to get Dr. Hopson for consultation. A messenger was also sent to the Uncompahgre agency to summon Dr. Lacey, Ouray's personal physician. National attention immediately focused on Ouray's illness because it was feared that the Utes would not sign the treaty if Ouray died.

Ouray's condition continued to get worse. A **Denver Times** special from the Uncompahgre agency, dated August 20, 1880,

reported:

> Indian runners from the Southern Ute agency arrived this morning, and report Chief Ouray dangerously ill and not expected to live. They came with a message from Ouray to agency physician here, Dr. Lacey, in whom he has the utmost confidence, requesting him to come immediately ... The Indians will furnish relays of horses, and the doctor intends to make a distance of one hundred and twenty miles in fifteen hours. Ouray went to that point to assist the commission in prevailing upon the Utes to sign the treaty: if Ouray dies, the treaty will never be signed by the White River Utes.

Dr. Hopson came from Animas City in response to Page's request, but he was of the opinion that little could be done in the way of treatment. On August 21, 1880, the **Times** correspondent telegraphed, "Ouray much worse and not expected to live. Interest in his condition nationwide."

S.B. Beaumont wrote to **The Denver Tribune** that same day:

> When I left the Southern Ute agency on the 20th there was grave apprehension on the part of the Commissioners that success in concluding the treaty depended largely upon Ouray's recovery, and his illness was regarded with serious alarm. My knowledge of the Southern Utes induces me to believe that they will not be influenced to decline the treaty by the death of the Uncompahgre Chief, and that if any serious difficulty arises it will come from the White River bands.

Chief Ignacio of the Weeminuche Utes probably had this photo taken when he was chief of police at a salary of $10 per month. It shows him well along in years compared to the 1880 picture taken in Washington. The tribe over which he presided still lives at Towaoc, where he chose to remain after refusing the offer of the United States government to accept farms in "severalty." He and his followers preferred to live in the communal style to which they were accustomed. Today, that band is known as the Ute Mountain Utes because their reservation is bounded on the west by the "Sleeping Ute" or "Ute Mountain." The other band of Southern Utes, the Capote, did accept the individual farm system and now live on the eastern end of the Ute lands along the Colorado border, with their tribal headquarters, ironically at the town of Ignacio. (Denver Public Library)

Buckskin Charlie was the last traditional chief of the Capote band of Utes. Charlie lived until May of 1936, achieving the age of ninety-six. His son, Antonio Buck, was elected the first tribal chairman. Chief Ouray, knowing that his time was growing short, requested that Buckskin Charlie be made head chief. Charlie, considerably younger than Ouray, was still his good friend, and Ouray had great faith in him. Buckskin Charlie spent the rest of his life justifying that faith. Never, with his knowledge, did any of his Indians commit any depredations against the white people in the region, although some white men did try to provoke an incident to justify removing the last of the Utes from Colorado. (Colorado Historical Society)

On Sunday evening, August 22nd, Dr. Lacey, of the Uncompahgre agency arrived. The Southern Ute agency doctor, Dr. Lacey, and Dr. Hopson all tried to treat Ouray while his medicine men were pounding his abdomen with their fists and bucking their heads against his chest to drive out the evil spirit. Lacey later reported that he felt Ouray died of a hernia which he neglected to treat because he was trying to get the treaty signed. The Ute medicine men had taken charge of Ouray's illness, and the white doctors realized there was not much they could do anyway. Ouray lingered in a comatose state from Saturday, August 21, until Tuesday, August 24, becoming lucid only occasionally for short periods.

Late Monday evening, August 23, it became evident that Ouray could not live for many more hours. Dr. Hopson gave up hope altogether and returned to Animas City. That same evening, **The Denver Tribune** correspondent wrote:

> Ouray is at the Southern Ute agency sick with Bright's Disease and will probably die before morning. It is likely his death will affect the treaty with the Southern Utes. No treaty has been signed yet.

On Tuesday, August 24, at eleven o'clock in the morning, an Indian arrived at the agency building and asked to see Dr. Lacey. He told the doctor to come at once, and the two immediately went to Ouray's tepee; but before they could enter, an Indian stepped out and silently motioned them back. Chief Ouray was dead.

A **Frank Leslies Illustrated Newspaper** correspondent filed the following report:

> Special from Los Pinos (Uncompahgre) Agency, Colorado, August 25, 1880: The death of Ouray on the 24th ... was a blow from which the Ute Nation will never recover. The greatest Indian that ever lived is dead. And there is no one to fill his place. The Utes seem to realize they have suffered an irreparable loss.

Special from Southern Ute Agency of the same date: As I telegraphed you yesterday, Ouray, the great chief of the Utes died. In one hour they had wrapped him in his blankets, tied him on one of his ponies, which was led by an Indian on horseback and

This group of men are at the original burial site of Chief Ouray on the occasion of his disinterment and reburial in the Ignacio cemetery. Buckskin Charlie (left) and another Indian at the front are holding a sack containing some of the great chief's bones. A myth that has circulated for many years is that Chief Ouray was secretly buried by the Indians and that they never would divulge the location to the white man. Some of these myths have even been developed since 1925, when his bones were disinterred and reburied—a well-publicized event. On that occasion, a four-day-long funeral was held, with both Christian and Indian rites, and was attended by a great throng of Indian and white people, many of them state and national dignitaries. (Colorado Historical Society)

followed by Chipeta and four other Indians, the procession moved quietly down the Pine River, to some secret spot, unknown, where he was buried with all his belongings and five horses were sacrificed near his grave. It is well that Ouray died away from his comfortable home in the Uncompahgre valley, which was well furnished, as all his articles would have been burned and sacrificed to this strange superstition of of the race. In the death of Ouray one of the historical characters of Colorado passes away. He has been featured for many years as the greatest Indian of his time and during his life has figured quite as prominently before the country as has any white man in the Rocky Mountains ... a man of pure instincts, of keen perception, and apparently possessed very proper ideas of justice and right—the friend of the white man and the protector of the Indian, ever boldly asserting the rights of his tribe and as continually doing all in his power to create favor for the whites with the Indians ... He dies as he has lived, in the mutual service of the Government and the Indians.

Some say Ouray's serious illness may have been aggravated by the certain depression he must have had because of the many lies told by the whites, the Meeker Massacre, and the impending removal of the Indians to Utah. There had definitely been a change in his attitude towards the white man. In the year or so before his death, he had reverted to Indian dress instead of his usual combination of Indian and white man's garb. He supposedly did not want the white doctors to treat him and told Chipeta and Buckskin Charlie as he was dying: "Hear me, both of you! Bury me where no white man will ever find my body. Bury me in a secret place." Perhaps the white man's food and ways had killed him. He is also quoted as saying "My Son!" several times before he died. Forty years later Buckskin Charlie said that the following conversation with Ouray also occurred:

When Chief Ouray was dying he told me there were several people coming from Washington—commissioner, inspectors and officers, also Secretary of the Interior, who were coming to talk about money which they would pay the Indians. "I am not going to live long and I want you as head of your tribe to sign, that seems when you sign you'll get paid every year. After you sign first, the rest of the tribe can sign, next the chief of the Kapoties, but the hardest one is the chief at Towaoc. I don't believe he will sign. We have good land here, plenty of water—don't let this land go. You stay here and take care of this land and work it. Buckskin Charlie, I don't want you to run around and leave your people. Stay until all your tribe dies and you die, too."

When Ouray died there were reportedly a thousand Indians camped near his tepee. Within a matter of minutes, nearly all of the Indians had supposedly moved at least a mile away because of their fear of the dead. Ouray's friends wrapped his body in new saddle blankets and buffalo robes, tied ropes and cords around it, and secured it to a horse. One of those present, Nathan Price, told the others in Chief Ouray's band that his father, Chief Suvata (Suyi-tah-ah), Chief of the Capote band, was buried on a rocky mesa two miles due south of Ignacio. He suggested that this would be a good place to bury Ouray where the white man couldn't find him, and that the two chiefs could be together. Chipeta, Chipeta's brother John McCook, Buckskin Charlie, Colorow, Naneese,

Joseph Price, and Nathan Price took Ouray's body to the suggested site and placed it in a natural cave under a huge rock on the mesa. His saddle was laid beside him and the entrance to the cave was then filled with rocks.

It was normal procedure for the Utes to secretly bury their dead in caves, along with their war equipment and personal effects. Very few white men had ever seen a Ute burial at the time of Ouray's death. The Utes dreaded being around a dead body, and burial was as hasty as possible. A death was immediately announced by the medicine man. Whatever clothes the dead man had on him were not removed; his limbs were straightened, his weapons were put beside him, then all were wrapped in blankets. A death song was usually kept up during this time. At the cave, the body was normally covered with stones to keep the animals away, and it was not unusual for two or more bodies to be in the same cave. The men, in the meanwhile, destroyed many of the personal effects and animals formerly owned by the dead man.

If Chipeta went through the usual mourning by a Ute widow, she would have smeared her face with charcoal and pitch. This would have been allowed to wear off naturally. As part of the mourning ritual, one of the Ute's horses was usually killed. In Ouray's case, one account says that three horses were slain, including a spotted one, but several other accounts say that five were destroyed.

The agent, officers, and other whites and Mexicans present at Ouray's death asked to go with the body for burial, but were refused. Immediately after his death, the Uncompahgre band requested his remains. The Southern Utes had no objections, and about two weeks after the burial they took some of the agency's officers, some of the U.S. commissioners, and others to the burial spot. They found the body to be in such a state of decomposition that it couldn't be removed. Ouray was to remain buried there for forty-five years.

Many felt that Ouray's death would doom the 1880 treaty. However, either fate or God took a hand: Chief Kaneache who had spoken against the treaty, was struck dead by lightening. Many Utes in the area at the time considered this an omen and signed the treaty; but still the requisite three-fourths had not ratified the document. Then Otto Mears rose (or sank, depending on one's point of view) to the occasion. He traveled the Ute territory, giving two dollars out of his own pocket to every Ute he could find who would sign the agreement. By September 11, 1880, he had obtained the necessary number of signatures. Included among the 110 signatures were those of Utes who took the names of all five commissioners, the Secretary of the Interior (Carl Schurz), San-a-vitch, and an Aleck Mears! The commissioners certified that the 110 signatures represented three-fourths of the adult Ute males out of the more than three thousand tribe members. When the chairman of the commission, George Manypenny, learned about Mears' tactics, he refused to endorse the treaty on the grounds that

Mears was guilty of bribery. Manypenny, and other commissioner Meacham, filed charges against Mears with Secretary Carl Schurz. However, that fall James A. Garfield was elected president, and Schurz was replaced by Samuel J. Kirkwood.

Nevertheless, in 1881, Mears was ordered to Washington to stand trial on the bribery charges. The investigation was held in the office of the Secretary of Interior. In the presence of the two Colorado senators, Henry M. Teller and N.P. Hill, Secretary Kirkwood asked Mears why he had given the Utes the two dollars each to sign the treaty. Mears replied that he had paid them the money because the Utes claimed that the two dollars in cash was worth more to them than the government's promise of fifty thousand dollars per year, which they would probably never get. "Was the money you paid them your own, or was it paid by the government?" Kirkwood

The lettering on this picture reads, "Cline's Ranch, Cimarron, Colo. Scene of the murder of young Jackson by the Ute Indians, 1880." There was a great outcry and angry demands from the whites in the area that the "foul murderers" of poor young Jackson be apprehended and executed. In fact, the Utes were retaliating for young Jackson's unprovoked killing of a young Indian, son of Chief Shavano; that act evidently wasn't considered a crime. Cline's Ranch was owned by Captain Cline, who was one of the founders and the first mayor of the town of Ouray. He was a member of the rescue party that went after the women hostages during the Meeker affair. He was accused of aiding the Indians when he set out to escort young Jackson to Gunnison to be tried for the murder. (Colorado Historical Society)

Barely six weeks after the death of Chief Ouray, Johnson Shavano and Indian Henry, both shown here with an unknown white man, were shot by a freighter named Jackson. The Utes immediately demanded that Jackson be arrested, which was done by soldiers from Fort Crawford. A detail of soldiers and numerous Indians set out with Jackson for Gunnison, the location of the nearest federal court. Jackson was to be held there until he could be tried for the murder of the young Indian. En route, the Indians, having lost faith in the white man's justice, forcibly wrestled the prisoner from the soldiers and administered their own justice, thus adding one more "incident" for the white man to use in persuading the federal government to repudiate the 1873 treaty and remove all the Utes from Colorado. (Denver Public Library)

asked. "I paid it out of my own pocket," Mears replied. "How much did it cost you?" Kirkwood asked. "Twenty-eight hundred dollars," replied Mears. "Send me a bill for it," Kirkwood said, "and I will see to it that the government reimburses you. You did a good job and I am grateful," Kirkwood continued. "I know a little about Indian character too, and I think that you were perfectly right in handling this matter as you did. Can you remove the Utes as the treaty specified?" Mears replied, "Yes, if you give me enough troops and keep Manypenny and Meacham out of the way."

On September 29, 1880, an incident occurred which not only threatened to nullify the Treaty of 1880, but also came very close to starting a major war. John H. Jackson, his nephew, Andrew Jackson, and a man named Mannell left Saguache with a load of whiskey for the town of Ouray. While they were eating dinner, two Utes—Johnson Shavano (son of Chief Shavano) and Indian Henry—rode into the camp and asked for food. Evidently, the Jacksons fired on the Utes, although the whites said that Johnson Shavano fired first. At any rate, Johnson was killed and Indian Henry was shot in the arm. The Ute version that the whites shot first is quite possibly correct because several people had previously seen the whites and that they had been drinking heavily.

The whites who were involved fled to H.C. Clines's ranch near present day Cimarron. Johnson's father went to Indian agent William Berry at the Uncompahgre agency and demanded that the murderer be punished immediately. Berry and several other whites went to Cline's ranch and put Jackson under arrest. The other white men in the area were furious that Jackson had endangered their lives by what he did. On October 1, Jackson was taken to Gunnison to be tried, but about sixty Indians ambushed the party and shot Jackson. The general feeling of the whites then swung against the Indians. Unfounded rumors circulated that Jackson had been tortured. Indian agent Berry and four other whites were blamed for letting the Utes do what they did. All five men were eventually arrested, but none was ever tried. The incident had only served to give the whites another excuse to get the Utes out of Colorado.

The next task of the Ute Indian commission was to determine exactly where the new reservation should be. Again Meacham and Manypenny opposed Mears. The exact words of the treaty were: "The Uncompahgre Utes agree to remove and settle upon agricultural lands on the Grand River near the mouth of the Gunnison River in Colorado, if a sufficient quantity of agricultural land shall be found there; if not, then upon such other unoccupied agricultural lands as may be found in that vicinity and in the Territory of Utah." Other parts of the treaty refer only to the junction of the rivers and omit any reference at all to Utah. Meacham and Manypenny said it was therefore obvious where the Utes should be moved.

Mears took a more liberal interpretation of the treaty, arguing that it gave the commission the right to move them all the way into Utah, whether or not enough agricultural land was in the area where the two rivers meet. He took the view that there was no good agricultural land there, even though that was one of the very reasons the whites wanted the land in the first place. Commissioners Russell and Bowman supported Mears.

The vote of the commission was three to two in favor of the Mears' interpretation. It is strange that Grand Junction, the largest city on the Western Slope of Colorado, now stands on the spot that was rejected as too barren for the Utes. Mears is quoted as having later said that he knew the region was fertile and that farmers would ultimately have demanded the land. He claimed that he was only trying to avoid another confrontation.

Upon examining Utah territory, Mears and the others decided to establish the new reservation southeast of the Uintah Reservation, where the Duchesne and White rivers enter the Green River. So, as a result of the Treaty of 1880, both the White River Utes and the Uncompahgre Utes were compelled to leave western Colorado.

Mears was also commissioned to supply the new agency and new agency buildings in Utah. Although it might be claimed that Mears was taking advantage of the Utes, in fact, he was being criticized by the whites as pro-Indian. Dave Day of **The Solid Muldoon** in Ouray, Colorado, wrote, "Otto Mears is not really a Ute. It is his complexion that makes him look that way."

Because of the Meeker Massacre, Colonel Ranold S. MacKenzie was sent from Fort Garland to the Uncompahgre agency with the Fourth Cavalry and nine companies of infantry. He arrived at the agency on May 25, 1880, and the soldiers immediately began patrols up and down the Uncompahgre and Gunnison rivers. A temporary supply camp known as the Cantonment on the Uncompahgre was finished on July 21, 1880, near the west bank of the Uncompahgre River about four miles north of the agency.

Shortly before the Utes' departure for Colorado, General MacKenzie, assembled the White River and Uncompahgre Utes near present day Olathe. The general had nine companies of cavalry and nine of infantry. The Utes made all kinds of excuses to delay their departure. They pleaded for more time to gather their animals and said that they wanted to go to the Yampa River to kill sufficient game for the coming winter. They begged to go to Cow Creek and to the Cimarron. MacKenzie had already given the Indians an extension of time, but he eventually gave them ten more days in which to attend to the matters they had requested. He told them that they had better then be prepared to leave.

Colorow, who had generally taken over as head Ute chief, was camped during this time a short distance away from MacKenzie's headquarters. As a safety precaution, MacKenzie had soldiers stationed on bluffs next to Colorow's camp to keep him and his followers under continual observation. Evidently, whiskey was smuggled to the Indians (which they no doubt drank plenty of, under the circumstances), and they became reckless.

After a week, the drunken Utes started a charge on MacKenzie's camp. However, the soldiers on the bluffs blew bugles and shot rockets to sound the alarm, and when Colorow and his followers came into view, they were met by four companies of cavalry. The Utes instantly stopped, had a short talk, then beat a hasty retreat

The log building shown here on the left is the Grand Junction Town Company office in 1883, where immigrants could purchase town lots. It was built shortly after the exodus of the Utes in September of 1881. The land was not legally open to white settlement until January 1, 1882, but there is some speculation that the log building may have been built a bit earlier than that. The Ute's campfires were scarcely cool before the entire region was overrun by white men seeking land for farms, ranches, or towns; then came the big promotion, with efforts to attract industry or anything else that would produce money and make the place grow. Some of the towns didn't make it, but others grew to be fairly large, prosperous, and permanent. (Colorado Historical Society)

back to their own camp.

That night General MacKenzie sent for two of the Indian commissioners and informed them of Colorow's attempted attack. He wanted to immediately move the Indians before there was any more trouble. The two commissioners signed the order for removal, and MacKenzie gave the Utes two hours to start for the reservation. He emphasized this order by placing six pieces of artillery on a hill overlooking the Ute camp. When the two hours were up, about fourteen hundred of the Utes began their long trek to their new reservation in northeastern Utah. They had already received sufficient rations at the Uncompahgre agency to take them on their journey. About ten thousand sheep and goats and several thousand horses were also taken, but many of the animals were lost before the Utes made it to their new reservation.

General MacKenzie escorted the Utes down the Uncompahgre River to the Gunnison River, which they then followed to the Grand

The large building to the left of center in this photo is the guard house at Fort Crawford. To its left is the hospital, and at the far right is the bakery. At first, it was simply called the "Cantonment on the Uncompahgre." On May 12, 1884, by presidential order, it was given the name of "Fort Crawford," in memory of Captain Emmet Crawford, killed by Apaches in Arizona. The cantonment, midway between the Los Pinos agency and Chief Ouray's permanent camp on the Uncompahgre, was established after the Meeker Incident to keep the Indians from going on the warpath. Although the Indians were moved to Utah in September of 1881, the cantonment remained for nine more years before it was closed because there was no longer any military need for it. (Colorado Historical Society)

River. On September 1, 1881, near present day Grand Junction, the Utes and their property were ferried across the Grand River in large boats. The boats remained there for many years, and travelers and settlers often made use of them to cross the river. On September 7, 1881, the last group made its exodus from western Colorado, which was now totally opened for settlement. General John Pope, MacKenzie's commander, wrote that "the whites who had collected, in view of [the Utes] removal were so eager and unrestrained by common decency that it was absolutely necessary to use military force to keep them off the reservation until the Indians were fairly gone ..."

The Utes arrived on September 13 at what was to be called the Ouray agency in honor of their late chief. It was not until January 5, 1882, that an executive order was signed, officially establishing the reservation for Tabeguache Utes in Utah. The Southern Utes were also to have moved to agricultural lands on the La Plata River, but it was eventually determined that they should stay on their 15 x 110-mile reservation. The reason given was the lack of sufficient agricultural land in the La Plata region, but it is clear that the whites wished to keep that area for themselves.

On September 12, 1881, the **Ouray Times** reported:

This artist's drawing depicts the Utes being ferried across the Grand (now Colorado) River as they were being moved into Utah Territory in August of 1881. This crossing was made near the confluence of the Grand and Gunnison rivers where the city of Grand Junction now stands. For many years afterwards, white settlers used the same boats to cross the Grand. The Treaty of 1880 provided that the Indians might be settled in that region on the Grand River "if sufficient agricultural land should be found there." The "experts" decided that the land was no good, so the Utes were driven into Utah Territory. The white man was then compelled to accept that "poor" land, upon which they built the largest city in western Colorado, planted thousands of fruit trees and grew crops of hay, grain, and garden produce. (Colorado Historical Society)

Chief Colorow, famous for his profound stubborness and resistance to this removal, was the last to leave the valley—a dull, prosaic dash of copper at the end of a long Indian sentence. Sunday morning the Utes bid adieu to their old hunting grounds—this is an event that has long devotedly been prayed for by our people. How joyful it sounds and with what satisfaction one can say, "The Utes have gone."

A Del Norte newspaper expressed a similar sentiment in verse:
Then shout the glad tidings
Triumphantly sing
The San Juan is opened
We've busted the ring.

Chapter Eleven

CHIPETA'S LAST DAYS— OURAY'S REBURIAL

Chief Ouray had always worried about Chipeta's future after his death, and for good reason. When the Utes were removed, she begged to be allowed to stay at her Uncompahgre farm, but the government wouldn't listen. So Chipeta was included among the 1,458 Uncompahgre Utes who left for Utah in September of 1881. For decades the whites had been trying to force the Utes into becoming farmers; now they were sending them to an arid land where there was no irrigation water available. One agent reported the land to be "... (the land is) extremely rugged and fearfully riven, being pinnacled with mountains, crags, and cliffs and torn with canons, arroyos, and ravines ... a wild and ragged desolation, valuable for nothing unless it shall be found to contain mineral deposits." The United States decided to sell Ouray and Chipeta's farm and use the proceeds for her future life. Most of the couple's personal effects and furniture were sold. Otto Mears bought a portion of the old homestead at a bargain price, but was ordered to reimburse Chipeta seven hundred dollars for improvements Ouray had made to the farm. Chipeta later gave away most of the money.

While Mears was at the agency, Chief Cojoe tried to murder him, claiming that he was the main reason the Utes were removed from Colorado. Mears finally resigned from the commission in April of 1882.

When first removed to Utah, Chipeta was promised by the federal government that she would receive a house as well built and furnished as her old one at the Uncompahgre agency. Instead, she was given a small, two-room dwelling that was never furnished or plastered and had no irrigation water for her small garden. Eventually, Chipeta gave up many of the ways of the whites, living most of her remaining years in a tepee. Ironically, she later received many gifts, such as fine china, which she couldn't use.

On April 1, 1888, **The Denver Republican** reported that Chipeta had remarried at the Ouray agency in Utah. Her new husband was supposedly "Toomuchagut," a White River Ute described as "a bloodthirsty savage" by one source and "quiet, friendly and wealthy" by another. The name of her new husband (Too-much-a-gut) seems too farcical to be true; it is likely that the story was a mere concoction by a newspaper writer who wanted to poke fun at the Utes. Chipeta and her husband were supposed to have joined

This group of Utes was photographed at Bitter Creek, Utah, where Chipeta spent the remainder of her life after the Utes were banished from western Colorado. She is fifth from the right in this picture. Of course, Chipeta was not confined solely to the reservation, and she made many trips into Colorado throughout the years. This, however, was her home in later life. Note the fine forest on the mountainside and the lush growth on the valley floor. Here, the Indians could graze a few sheep, which they could fatten on thistles and so provide rich mutton for food, and wool for skins and clothing. How fortunate they were not to have been compelled to settle in the Grand River Valley in Colorado. (Denver Public Library)

Colorow's band. However, there have been no other references to Toomuchagut, and if she did indeed remarry, it must have been a very brief affair. Several other unsubstantiated reports that Chipeta had remarried were made at various times later in her life.

In fact, Chipeta had a lonely existence. She suffered from rheumatism and often went to the Glenwood Hot Springs to ease her arthritis pain. Her brother, Sapovanero, succeeded Ouray so she was still well treated by the tribe, but the white man forgot her for the time being.

The Utes did have one more "war" during Chipeta's lifetime. Because game was insufficient at their reservation, the Utes were allowed to roam eastward into Colorado. Many small incidents occurred with both whites and Utes being killed. Then in late July of 1887, a Ute named Augustine was shot at by whites near Rangely in northwestern Colorado. The exact reasons for the shooting are not known, but evidently the Utes were committing a game violation.

This 1907 photograph of Chipeta was taken in Montrose by a photographer named McKee. Chipeta was there by invitation on several occasions, such as the Montrose County Fair. In her later life, she became kind of a folk heroine, and everyone wanted his or her picture taken with her. Some of the Indian blankets she is posing with may have been Navajo or government-issued, but the water baskets were made by the Utes, who applied a coating of warm pine pitch to the inside of woven dried willow twigs. The Utes also made fine leather, tanned-skin clothing, and other useful things from the hides of the animals they killed for meat. There was much bartering between the many tribes, the products of one traded for those of another. (Colorado Historical Society)

Colorow and his band of about a dozen men with their women and children went to Meeker to investigate the shooting.

While on their way, it was reported that they were stealing horses. The whites were scared of reprisals, and stories of invading Ute bands soon spread. Garfield County Sheriff, Jim Kendall, seeking to become a hero by chasing "dangerous Indians" out of Colorado, came across the Ute squaws picking berries and made lewd and threatening remarks to them. Chipeta herself is supposed to have run him off at gun point. Later an angry argument between the Ute men and the sheriff's posse ended when one of the sheriff's

Chipeta often came through the city of Ouray while traveling to Ignacio to visit the Southern Utes (or perhaps secretly to visit Ouray's grave). The August 1, 1913 issue of "The Ouray Plaindealer" reported that "accompanied by four bucks, five squaws and a single papoose the famous Chipeta visited her husband's old hunting place here last Sunday. The band was entertained by the Commercial Club and gave a full dress parade on Main Street in the afternoon. They were traveling south." A local photographer took this and a half dozen other photos of the occasion. (Colorado Historical Society)

men fired a gun. Immediately Colorow began moving his camp toward the safety of the Utah border, while the sheriff dramatically reported a total Ute uprising. Panic spread quickly. Ranchers left their homes, Governor Alva Adams sent in seven brigades of Colorado National Guard, and citizens and ranchers joined Sheriff Kendall's posse. Colorow's little band of Utes was intercepted just fifteen miles east of the Utah boundary. A skirmish followed, in which several soldiers were killed or wounded; a member of the posse was also killed. The Indians lost about a dozen men. A hundred Utah Utes came to the rescue of Colorow and his women and children, ushering them into Utah to higher ground, where they thought they would be safe.

The farce has been dubbed "The Colorow War" and cost the State of Colorado over eighty thousand dollars, in addition to the casualties suffered. A few days later Sheriff Kendall mysteriously disappeared. Foul play was suspected, but by that time no one really cared, and an investigation was never made.

Many of the Ute treaties were eventually broken. Payments were not paid, and further attempts were made to eliminate even the Uintah, Ouray, and Southern Ute agencies. But attitudes towards the Indians were changing. Public opinion finally recognized their mistreatment.

The biggest problem, however, came from the 1880 treaty requirement that the Utes be paid for the land sold to whites in western Colorado. Two suits were eventually brought for this money, and in 1911, three million dollars was recovered for the Utes. Almost every year, from 1886 to 1894, bills were introduced in Congress to move the Southern Utes out of Colorado, but they were all defeated.

In 1895, the Hunter Act set aside the Southern Ute reservation and provided that allotments of land could be made to the Utes individually. However, the tribes split over whether they wanted their people to have private ownership of land, with Ignacio and his

This was the scene on west Main Street in Montrose, Colorado on March 15, 1925, when Chipeta was reburied. The event was reportedly attended by five thousand people, and her body was interred in a concrete mausoleum on the farm that had been her home with Chief Ouray. Only forty-four years had passed since Chipeta, along with all her people, had been driven by the cavalry, as if they were cattle, from their home on the Uncompahgre to their new reservation in Utah. Now, Chipeta had a military honor guard accompany her body to its place of interment just beyond the Uncompahgre River south of Montrose. Attempts were made by various white people to get permission from the Indians at Ignacio to exhume the remains of the chief, now dead for forty-five years, but their efforts were unsuccessful. (Colorado Historical Society)

band favoring no allotments and moving to the west, near Ute Mountain, where a subagency was founded. Later the entire reservation was split into two parts. The western, or non-allotted part, became the Ute Mountain Reservation; the eastern part remained the Southern Ute Reservation.

Eventually (and symbolically), Chipeta ended up on Bitter Creek in the Ute Indian Reservation in Utah. There she became an Episcopalian about the turn of the century. **The Colorado Springs Gazette** of August 5, 1911, reported that a fund had been started for Chipeta and it was hoped that the government would better provide for her. It was also noted that she had been "exiled" to Utah and it was the hope of the contributors that she would be allowed to return to Colorado and the money used for her benefit. But Chipeta stayed in Utah. In 1912, Mrs. W. G. King met Chipeta and reported on her condition:

> Chipeta, Ouray's widow, was among the first Indians to come to our home. Her eyes were getting bad, and she was worried about them. A doctor in Grand Junction, Colorado, had removed a cataract from one eye. One day Chipeta came in to see me about her eyes. I telephoned to her doctor, and he gave me instructions for treatments. Hot packs were to be put on her eyes, and he sent medicine to be dropped into them.
>
> I explained she must have treatment for a long period of time in order to get relief and to have improved eyesight. The Indians were very cooperative. They moved down from their camp on Bitter Creek, and made camp up on "Vack Creek," a short way from Dragon. At last the eye treatments for Chipeta were over and her eyes were improved. Our Indians moved back to Bitter Creek where the summer Indian camps were.

Even after a cataract operation in 1913, Chipeta's eyes were bad enough that when she was indoors she needed to be told the colors of the beads that she used for the beautiful beadwork she made; only when she was outdoors could she differentiate the colors.

Chipeta would often travel from Utah back to Montrose, or even much farther south to Ignacio. The Indians from the Utah reservation at Fort Duchesne especially liked to attend the Montrose county fair. The locals noted that Chipeta would often go out to the river where her former farm was located, sometimes returning with tears on her face. On September 28, 1921, the Montrose paper reported that Chipeta came to Montrose when President Taft attended the opening of the Gunnison Tunnel.

In 1913, Chipeta visited the town of Ouray. The August 1 issue of the local paper described her stopover:

> Accompanied by four bucks, five squaws, a little

The bones of Chief Ouray were recovered from their original burial site in 1925 by the Utes. At the time of Ouray's death in 1880, the Indians did not bury their dead in cemeteries, as was the white man's custom. Ouray was buried in a rock crevice, then sealed in with rocks and mud to keep scavenging animals from reaching his remains. After Ouray's remains were exhumed, four Indians who had assisted with the original burial forty-five years before served as pallbearers during the four days of rites and the reburial in the cemetery at Ignacio. The authenticity of Ouray's remains was established in affidavits given by Buckskin Charlie, Joseph Price, John McCook, and Naneese, who were among the six men who had helped Chipeta bury Ouray the first time. (Colorado Historical Society)

girl and a single papoose, the famous Chipeta visited her husband's old hunting place here last Sunday. The band was entertained by the Commercial Club and gave a full dress parade on Main Street in the afternoon. They were traveling south.

A photo was taken of the group on the steps of the Ouray Elks Club. It was reported that Chipeta, Buckskin Charlie, Mountain Sheep, three squaws, and a little girl named Mamie were lodged and fed at the Beaumont Hotel. The city band played for her in front of the hotel, and later the entire Ute group saw a "picture show," which all the Indians enjoyed.

A story is told of Cato Sells, the Superintendent of Indian Affairs in 1916. It seemed he was informed that Chipeta, now seventy-three years old, had been sadly neglected. He decided that the United States government had not shown a proper appreciation of her for her many services and great distinction as the celebrated wife of Chief Ouray. He wanted to do something for her while she was still alive. Traveling to Utah he found Chipeta living with a small group of nomadic Utes who kept about a thousand sheep and some thirty cattle pastured during the summer at the head of Bitter Creek. Sells asked Chipeta if there was anything she would like the government to do for her. Through an interpreter she replied, "I desire nothing; what is good enough for my people is good enough for me. And I expect to die very soon." She also made the following statement:

> Never have I had an unkind feeling or an unkind thought toward the Government in Washington, and if I were to express what I have in my mind, someone would misunderstand and think that Chipeta's heart has changed and that she is no longer friendly toward the Government.

Cato Sells discussed the matter with the reservation agent, who pointed out that at various times during her life on the reservation in Utah, Chipeta had been given gifts from white admirers. Most of them she had not known how to use. Once, she was given some fifty- and some one-hundred-dollar bills, but she did not realize their value and merely passed the green paper on to her friends. On another occasion, she received a trunk filled with beautiful silks, and again gave most of them away. Then another time, she was given a valuable set of china, but it was later found unused at her summer camp on Bitter Creek because she much preferred enamelware. The agent suggested and Sells subsequently purchased a gaily-covered shawl as an appropriate gift.

In her old age, Chipeta became almost totally blind from her cataracts. Her eyesight was so bad that she even had to follow a cord stretched from her tepee into the brush to relieve herself. She was later operated on again in Grand Junction for her cataracts, but without success. The widow of General Charles Adams, former Indian agent and commissioner, located Chipeta and wrote that she

This photograph was made May 24, 1925, during the reburial rites for Chief Ouray. The first four men, from left to right, are Naneese, John McCook, Joseph Price, and Buckskin Charlie—all four assisted at the original burial in 1880. Now, in 1925, they again serve as pallbearers at the four-day Indian and Christian burial rites. The other four perhaps served as an "honor guard" accompanying the great chief to his "final" resting place. All eight, wearing their finest ceremonial attire with headdresses made of eagles' feathers, posed for this picture in front of the Consolidated Ute Agency at Ignacio, which was headquarters for the Capote band of Southern Utes. (Denver Public Library)

was "living on a barren bit of Utah land where even the experienced farmer could not make a living much less an old woman ... She was clever at making certain things, but it is late in the day for her to learn to till the ground where Uncle Sam has placed her and said make a living or starve. Winter is coming on. Her little log house should be more comfortable."

Chipeta died on August 16, 1924, at Bitter Creek. She was eighty-one years old, poor, unhappy, and nearly blind. She died of chronic gastritis, having outlived Ouray by over 40 years. After her death, what was left of Chipeta and Ouray's furniture and personal possessions was sold for a pittance. Chipeta was buried on the Uintah Indian reservation in a shallow grave at the bottom of a little sand wash. It was a tragic end for one called "the laughing maiden of the Utes."

Shortly before Chipeta's death, L. M. Wayt, a white trader on the Ute Reservation at Ignacio, had begun talking with Buckskin Charlie about erecting a monument on Chief Ouray's grave.

This is only a small part of the procession approaching the cemetery at the 1925 burial rites for Chief Ouray. Ouray's remains ride in the pickup truck with the brush piled on the back, shading the coffin. Perhaps the brush covering had some cultural or spiritual significance. The Indians on horseback, wearing the ceremonial headdresses, are part of the honor guard. What a difference this was from the first burial, which was done hurriedly, with Ouray's body being secured to the back of an Indian pony for the ride to the burial place. At last, the great Chief Ouray received a burial befitting his true stature among men, both Indian and white. (Colorado Historical Society)

Buckskin Charlie agreed that a monument was needed and had his nephew, Babe Watts, show Wayt where Ouray's secret burial spot was located. The men unearthed two shoulder blades, two ribs and an arm bone; these they reburied. When Chipeta died in 1924, the location of Ouray's body was revealed also to E. E. McKean, the superintendent of the Consolidated Ute Indian agency at Ignacio. McKean requested that the federal government appropriate money for a monument and began to make plans for the reburial of Ouray. He also wanted Chipeta's body to be brought from Utah and reinterred next to Ouray's new grave.

Shortly after Chipeta's death, Albert Reagan discovered her grave in Utah and suggested to John McCook, her brother, that her remains be moved to a better location, since coyotes had been digging at the gravesite and there was also the threat of the body being washed away. In the meanwhile a group of Montrose citizens wanted Chipeta's body brought back to Colorado to be buried at Ouray's old farm. McCook gave his consent, and the Indian agent,

F. A. Gross, made arrangements for the transfer of the body. On March 3, 1925, C. E. Adams, the editor of the Montrose newspaper, received a letter from agent Gross saying that Chipeta's body had been exhumed and was ready for shipment. However, the mausoleum at Montrose was still incomplete. Gross wrote Adams that the construction should be hurried since it would make a bad impression on McCook and the other Utes if they arrived and had to await completion of the vault. Adams responded:

F.A. Gross, Supt.
Fort Duchesne, Utah

Dear Sir:

> Men at work on tomb. Weather fierce, but we will have it ready. Wire when you start or when ready. We want to make the Indians feel we are in earnest and thereby inspire them to make a diligent search for enough of Ouray's remains to make a tomb for him (also). Better wire.

C.E. Adams
Montrose, Colorado

The body of Chipeta arrived at Montrose on March 15, 1925, accompanied by Hugh Owens, who was the agricultural agent of the Indian agency at Fort Duchesne, and Reverend M. J. Hersey, a minister who represented F. A. Gross and who had received Chipeta into the Episcopal Church twenty-seven years before. John McCook and another Ute by the name of Yagnah also accompanied the body. That afternoon Chipeta's body was taken to the Ouray Memorial Park and reburied. During an elaborate ceremony, before almost five thousand people, Reverend Hersey, McCook and many other dignitaries spoke of Chipeta's loyalty and bravery. The procession that followed her casket was reported to be a mile long.

The Montrose citizens then wanted Ouray to be reburied next to Chipeta, and McCook was sent to Ignacio to try to obtain any necessary permission. He met with failure, although some accounts indicate that he may not have tried very hard to push for the relocation. However, his request did spur the Southern Utes into action. Buckskin Charlie, Wayt, and a newspaper reporter and photographer went to Ouray's secret burial spot and removed the bones that had earlier been reburied. Because the burial spot was in an arroyo, it was not possible to locate all the remains, and no one could really be sure that what they found were the bones of Ouray and not Suvata. It is quite possible that many of the bones had been washed away or picked up by whites who came through the area.

Earlier, a rumor had been spread that Ouray was buried in the San Miguel Mountains. Some, therefore, questioned whether the

This photograph was taken in 1937 at the burial of John McCook beside the sarcophagus of his sister Chipeta at the old Ouray homestead. Cheta, sister of Chipeta and McCook, says a final good-bye to her brother before his coffin is lowered into the grave. Note the scores of local school children let out for the occasion. Chipeta's and McCook's graves are within a few paces of the Ute Historical Museum. Chipeta's sarcophagus rests on top of the ground, while McCook's is the traditional white man's grave. Just below the museum ground, adjacent to the parking area at the side of the road, is a cold-water spring housed under a concrete tepee. Ouray and Chipeta obtained their drinking and cooking water from this spring. (Denver Public Library)

Here, in a neat, attractive little cemetery, with many white crosses and occasional granite markers, a pair of tall monuments memorialize two great and beloved chiefs, Ouray and Buckskin Charlie. The peaceful look of this scene suggests that many Indians have at last reached a place with the Great Spirit, where never again will the white man encroach upon their lands. (Colorado Historical Society)

bones at Ignacio were really those of Chief Ouray. However, when Ouray was reinterred some forty-five years after his death, four of the Utes who had been in the original burial party swore in affidavits that the bones that were found two miles south of Ignacio and reburied were actually those of Ouray.

Buckskin Charlie, Joseph Price, John McCook, and Naneese all supervised the removal of Ouray's remains and the reburial at the cemetery near the Ignacio agency. Colorow, Babe Watts, and L. M. Wayt also confirmed the bones to be those of Ouray. It was also now evident that Chipeta had been coming back regularly to Ignacio, primarily to visit the original gravesite, although she did have some distant relatives who lived at the agency.

Another rumor still exists. The story is told that shortly before Ouray died, he gave Chipeta a large sack of gold and silver. (Payments from the United States to the Indians were made by gold and silver coins at that time.) Chipeta is supposed to have thrown the sack in the Pine River because she was so disgusted with the whites. Needless to say, the money has never been found.

Ouray's reburial on May 24, 1925, included an Indian ceremony that lasted four days, followed by a Christian service that was half-Catholic and half-Protestant. This occurred because of a dispute over Ouray's religion. With Solomon-like wisdom, a section of the fence that divided the Protestant and Catholic portions of the cemetery was removed so that Ouray could be reburied one-half on each side. The fence posts still remain, making it clear that the controversy did exist.

The ceremonies were attended by the largest group of whites and Indians to assemble on the Southern Ute agency up to that time. A simple cement headstone made by the Utes marks the grave. Later, in 1939, a monument was built at Ignacio to honor Ouray, Severo, Ignacio, and Buckskin Charlie. It is eight feet square at the base, five feet square at the top, and eighteen feet high, with busts of the four Indians located on its sides.

Chipeta's grave is now the site of the Ouray Memorial Park. The park is a nine-acre historic shrine maintained by the State Historical Society and located near the couple's old farm immediately south of Montrose. A tall monument with a bust of Ouray has been erected on the spot, and a cement tepee has been built over the farm's spring. The adobe house that Ouray lived in stood for quite some time to the west of the tepee, but in 1944, part of the house burned and the remains were torn down. John McCook was buried along side his sister Chipeta in 1937. It is somehow fitting that Colorado's largest and finest tribute to any Indian or Indian tribe is located at this spot—a site first given to Ouray and Chipeta, then taken away from them, and finally dedicated to their memory.

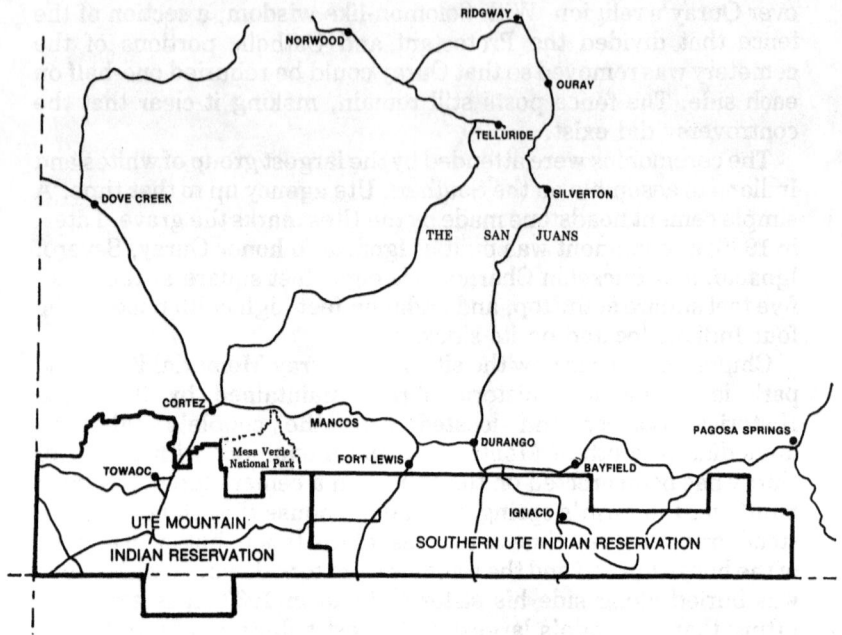

UTE MOUNTAIN AND SOUTHERN UTE RESERVATIONS TODAY

What was originally one long, narrow reservation in the southwestern corner of Colorado has now been cut up and maneuvered so that a part of the Ute Mountain Reservation even extends into New Mexico. In 1895, the Hunter Act made allotments of individual land available to the Indians instead of having them hold it collectively, as a tribe. The Ute Mountain Utes decided to stay with the old way, but the Southern Utes went with individual ownership. After the Southern Utes took 160 acres apiece, the balance was thrown open to whites, but some land went unclaimed and reverted to the Southern Ute tribe as a whole. The result is that the Southern Ute Reservation actually looks like a piece of Swiss cheese.

EPILOGUE

Ouray's obituary in **The Denver Tribune** read in part:
In the death of Ouray, one of the historical characters of Colorado passes away. He has figured for many years as the greatest Indian of his time, and during his life has figured quite as prominently before the country as has any white man in the Rocky Mountains. It is therefore meet and proper that on the occasion of his death, his life should be remembered. The record of his deed is one of simple parts, yet he has proven himself elevated so far above other men of his race and time that his acts stand out in bold relief. Ouray is in many respects—indeed, we may say in all respects—a remarkable Indian; a man of pure instincts, of keen perception, and apparently possesses very proper ideas of justice and right, the friend of the white man and the protector of the Indian, ever standing up and boldly asserting the rights of his tribe, and as continually doing all in his power to create favor for the white man with the Indians.

Today, in Colorado, a town, a county, a mountain, and dozens of small camps and ranches are named after Chief Ouray. It is always with reverent, hushed tones that his name is mentioned. "Remarkable," "brave," "honest," "sincere," "refined," "polished" and "courageous" are just a few of the adjectives that precede his name.

Ouray lived in a time when the typical American thought of Indians as savages living in a subhuman manner. The United States government was determined to destroy the Utes' livelihood and culture and was astonished and enraged when the Indians fought back. At the same time, many of the whites who were so pompous were themselves lying to and cheating the Indians. Sometimes we have to ask ourselves who the real savages were.

Ouray became the chief of the Ute Nation at a time when his race was destined to be overrun by the white man. Prior to Ouray's time, the Indian was perhaps the most independent human on earth. He was truly in tune with nature and accepted life as he found it. But his centuries-old way of life was coming to an end. Whether the Meeker Massacre had occurred or not, the Utes were destined to leave Colorado.

Most Indian chiefs such as Geronimo, Red Cloud or Crazy Horse are known because of the wars they waged against the white man. Ouray gained his fame through his efforts for peace. It is a legacy that we often forget in modern times. Through skillful negotiations he was able to keep the white man out of Ute territory for decades after most of the other Indian tribes were living on small reservations. But Ouray also realized the ultimate destiny of his people: they had to submit to the whites. It hurt him deeply that he was lied to and his people were mistreated by the white man. At the end of his life, he probably didn't want the burden of the position that had been thrust upon him. The story of Ouray is the story of the American Indian. He was befriended, mistreated and betrayed — then forgotten when his usefulness was over.

BIBLIOGRAPHY

Athearn, Robt. G., **The Coloradans.** Albuquerque: University of New Mexico Press, 1976.

Atwood, Wallace, **The Rocky Mountains.** New York: The Vanguard Press, 1945.

Baker, James H. and Le Roy R. Hafen, Editor, **History of Colorado.** Denver: Linderman Co., Inc., 1927, Vol. I.

Beckner, Ray, **Guns Along the Silver San Juan.** Canon City, Colorado: Master Printers, 1975.

Bluemel, Elinor, **One Hundred Years of Colorado Women.** Published by the author, 1973.

Borland, Lois, "The Sale of the San Juan," **Colorado Magazine.** Vol. 28, No. 2, April, 1951.

Bowles, Samuel, **The Switzerland of America.** Springfield, Mass.: Samuel Bowles and Co., 1869 (Reprint 1977, Clearing House Publications, Denver, Colo.)

Boyer, Warren, **Vanishing Trails of Romance.** Denver: Great West Publishers, 1923.

Brandes, T. Donald, **Military Posts of Colorado.** Ft. Collins, Colorado: The Old Army Press, 1973.

Brown, Robert L., **An Empire of Silver.** Caldwell, Idaho: The Caxton Printers, Ltd., 1968.

Bueler, Gladys R., **Colorado's Colorful Characters.** Golden, Colorado: The Smoking Stack Press, 1975.

Burt, Olive, **Ouray the Arrow.** New York, New York: Messnere, 1953.

Carhart, Arthur H., **Colorado.** New York: Coward-McCann, Inc., 1932.

Cerquone, Joseph, **In Behalf of the Light - The Dominguez and Escalante Expedition of 1776.** The Dominguez-Escalante Bicentennial Expedition, 1976.

Crampton, C. Gregory, "Indian Country," **Utah Historical Quarterly**, Spring, 1971, Vol. 39, No. 2.

Crum, Josie Moore, **Ouray County, Colorado**. Durango, Colorado: San Juan History, Inc., 1962.

D.A.R., Sarah Platt Decker Chapter, **Pioneers of the San Juan Country**. Colorado Springs, Colo.: Outwest Printing Co., 1942, Vol. I.

Daniels, Helen Sloan, compiler, **The Ute Indians of Southwestern Colorado**. Durango, Colorado: Durango Public Library Museum Project National Youth Administration, 1941.

Darley, Rev. George M., **Pioneering in the San Juan**. Chicago: Fleming H. Revell, Co., 1899.

Dawson, Thomas F., "Major Thompson, Chief Ouray and the Utes," **Colorado Magazine**, Vol. 7., No. 3, May, 1930

Dawson, Thomas F. and F.J.V. Skiff, **The Ute War: A History of the White River Massacre**. Denver: Tribune Publishing House, 1879.

Delaney, Robert W., "The Southern Utes a Century Ago," **Utah Historical Quarterly**, Spring 1971, Vol. 39, No. 2.

Delaney, Robert W., **The Southern Ute People**. Phoenix, Arizona: Indian Tribal Series, 1974.

Dorset, Phyllis F., **The New Eldorado - The Story of Colorado's Gold and Silver Rushes**. London: The Macmillan Co., 1970.

Downing, Finis E., "With the Ute Peace Delegation of 1863, Across the Plains and at Conejos," **Colorado Magazine**, Vol. 22, No. 5, September, 1945.

Dunklee, Edward V., "Colorado Cannibalism," **1946 Brand Book**. Denver, Colo.: The Westerners, 1947.

Dunn, William R., **War Drum Echos**. Colorado Springs: Century One Press, 1979.

Emmitt, Robert, **The Last War Trail: The Utes and the Settlement of Colorado**. Norman, Oklahoma: University of Oklahoma Press, 1954.

Fenwick, Robert W., **Alferd Packer - The True Story of the Maneater**. Denver, Colorado: Publishers Press of Denver, 1963.

Ferrell, Mallory Hope, **Silver San Juan**. Boulder, Colorado: Pruett Publishing Co. Press, 1952.

Frank Leslie's Illustrated Newspaper, Ouray Obituary, Sept. 18, 1880.

Guinn, Jack, "Ouray—Foresighted Chief," **Empire Magazine, The Denver Post**, May 1, 1966.

Hafen, Ann, **Quenched Fire and Other Poems.** Denver: The World Press Inc., 1937.

Hafen, LeRoy R., Editor, **Colorado and its People.** New York: Lewis Historical Publishing Co., Inc., 1948.

Hafen, LeRoy R., Editor, **The Mountain Men and the Fur Trade of the Far West, Vol. II.** Glendale, Calif.: The Arthur H. Clark Co., 1965.

Hafen, LeRoy R., "Ute Indians and the San Juan Mining Region," **Ute Indians,** Vol. 2, Clearwater Publishing Co., 1974.

Hafen, LeRoy R. and Ann Hafen, **Our State: Colorado.** Denver, Colorado: West Publishing Co., 1971.

Hall, Frank, **History of the State of Colorado.** Chicago: The Blakely Printing Company, 1890.

Harris, Henry, "The Indians and the Fur Men," **Utah Historical Quarterly.** Spring 1971, Vol. 39, No. 2.

Henderson, Junius, et al., **Colorado - Short Studies of its Past and Present.** Boulder: University of Colorado Press, 1927.

Hodge, Frederick Webb, editor, **Handbook of American Indians,** Smithsonian Institution, Bureau of American Ethrology, Bulletin 30, Washington Government Printing Office, 1910.

Howbert, Irving, **Indian of the Pikes Peak Region.** New York: The Knickerbocker Press, 1914.

Hughes, J. Donald, **American Indians in Colorado.** Boulder, Colorado: Pruett Publishing Co., 1977.

Hurt, Amy Passmore, "Ouray, The Arrow," **Real West Magazine,** Vol. XI No. 65, November, 1968.

Hunt, Inez and Wanetta W. Draper, **To Colorado's Restless Ghosts.** Denver, Colorado: Sage Books, 1960.

Jackson, Clarence, **Picture Maker of the Old West - William H. Jackson.** New York: Charles Scribner Sons, 1947.

Jackson, William Henry, **Time Exposure - The Autobiography of William Henry Jackson.** New York: Cooper Square Publishers, 1970.

Jackson, William Henry, **The Diaries of William Henry Jackson, Frontier Photographer.** Printed in LeRoy and Ann W. Hafen, **The Far West and the Rockies Historical Series.** Glendale, California: The Arthur H. Clark Company, 1957.

James, Gen. Thomas, **Three Years Among the Mexicans and the Indians.** Rio Grande Press, 1968 Reprint (1846 Original Edition).

Jefferson, J., R. Delaney and G. Thompson, **The Southern Utes.** Ignacio, Colorado: Southern Ute Tribe, 1972.

Jocknick, Sidney, **Early Days on the Western Slope of Colorado.** Glorieta, New Mexico: The Rio Grande Press, Inc., 1913.

Johnson, Jerome W., "Murder on the Uncompahgre," **Colorado Magazine.** Vol. 43, No. 2, Summer, 1966

Kaplan, Michael, **Otto Mears - Paradoxical Pathfinder.** Silverton, Colorado: San Juan County Book Co., 1982.

King, Mrs. W.G., "Our Ute Indians," **Colorado Magazine,** April 1960, Vol. XXXVII, Number 2.

Kushner, Ervan F., **Alferd G. Packer. Cannibal! Victim?** Frederick, Colorado: Platte N' Press, 1980.

Kushner, Ervan F., **Otto Mears: His Life & Times.** Frederick, Colorado: Jende-Hagan Bookcorp., 1979.

Lavender, David, **The Big Divide.** Garden City, N.Y.: Doubleday & Co., Inc., 1949.

Lavender, David, **The Rockies.** New York: Harper & Row, 1968.

Look, Al, **Utes' Last Stand.** Denver, Colorado: Golden Bell Press, 1972.

Lyman, June and Norma Denver, **Ute People, An Historical Study.** Salt Lake, Utah: University of Utah, 1970.

Mangan, Terry Wm., **Colorado on Glass.** Denver: Sundance, Ltd., 1975.

Marsh, Barton W., **The Uncompahgre Valley and the Gunnison Tunnel.** Montrose, Colo.: Marsh & Torrence, 1905.

Martin, Mary and Gene, **Colorado's Hall of Fame, A Quick Picture History.** Colorado Springs, Colorado: Little London Press, 1974.

Mazzulla, Fred and Jo, **Al Packer - A Colorado Cannibal.** Denver, Colorado: Published by authors, 1968.

McMechen, Edgar C., "Ouray Memorial Park Acquired by the State Historical Society," **Colorado Magazine.** Vol. 22, No. 4, July, 1945.

McClellan, Val J., **This Is Our Land.** New York: Vantage Press, Two Volumes, 1977.

Meeker, Josephine, **The Ute Massacre.** Vic Press, 1974. Reprint, Original Old Franklin Publishing, Philadelphia, Penn., 1879.

Miller, David E., editor, **The Route of the Dominguez - Escalante Expedition, 1776-77.** A Report of Trail Research Conducted Under the Auspices of the Dominguez - Escalante State/Federal Bicentennial Committee and the Four Corners Regional Commission, 1976.

Moody, Ralph, **The Old Trails West.** New York: Thomas Y. Crowell Company, 1963.

Nankiwell, Major John H., "Fort Crawford, Colorado, 1880-1890," **Colorado Magazine,** Vol. 11, No. 2, March, 1934.

Nankiwell, Major John H., **History of the Military Organizations of the State of Colorado.** Denver: Kistler Stationery Co., 1935.

O'Neil, Floyd A., "The Reluctant Suzerainty, the Unitah and Ouray Reservation," **Utah Historical Quarterly,** Spring 1971, Vol. 39, No. 2.

Ouray County Plaindealer, **Ouray Centennial-Historic Souvenir Issue,** Ouray, Colorado, 1976.

Perkins, Robert L., **The First Hundred Years.** Garden City, New York: Doubleday & Co., Inc., 1959.

Rathmell, Ruth, **Of Record and Reminiscence.** Ouray, Colorado: Ouray County Plaindealer & Herald, 1976.

Rathmell, Judge Wm., **History of Ouray County,** Unpublished Manuscript.

Reed, Vernon Z., "The Southern Ute Indians of Early Colorado," **The California Illustrated Magazine,** 1893.

Riddle, Jack P., "Besieged on Milk Creek," **Great Western Indian Fights.** Lincoln, Nebraska: University of Nebraska Press, 1960.

Ridgway, Arthur, "The Stoney Pass Road," **Colorado Magazine,** Vol. 16, No. 2, March, 1939.

Ripley, Henry and Martha, **Handclasp of East and West.** Denver: Williamson-Huffner Engraving and Printing Co., 1914.

Roberts, Dan, **A Story of the Centennial State.** Grand Junction, Colorado: Eagle Tail Press, 1973.

Rockwell, Wilson, "Portrait in the Gallery, Otto Mears—Pathfinder of the San Juans," **The 1967 Denver Westerners Brand Book.** Denver, Colorado: The Denver Westerners, Inc., Vol. 23, 1968.

Rockwell, Wilson, **Sunset Slope.** Denver: Big Mountain Press, 1956.

Rockwell, Wilson, **Uncompahgre Country.** Denver: Sage Books, 1965.

Rockwell, Wilson, **Uncompahgre Frontier.** Unpublished Manuscript in Mesa County Public Library, 1962.

Rockwell, Wilson, **The Utes a Forgotten People.** Denver, Colorado: Sage Books, 1956.

Roe, Frank Gilbert, **The Indian and the Horse.** Norman, Oklahoma: University of Oklahoma Press, 1955.

Saunders, William F., **The Joy of the Frontier.** An unpublished manuscript, a copy of which is owned by Marvin Gregory of Ouray, Colorado.

Schiel, Jacob H., **Journey Through The Rocky Mountains and the Humbolt Mountains to the Pacific Ocean.** Norman, Oklahoma: University of Oklahoma Press, (Reprint) 1959.

Schoolcraft, Henry R., **History of the Indian Tribes of the United States.** Philadelphia: Lippincott & Co., (Vol. 5) 1855.

Schroeder, Albert H., "A Brief History of the Southern Utes," **Southwestern Lore,** Vol. XXX, No. 4, March, 1964.

Sprague, Marshall, **Colorado, A Bicentennial History.** New York: W.W. Norton and Co., Inc., 1976.

Stacher, S.F., "Ouray and the Utes," **Colorado Magazine,** Vol. 27, No. 2, April, 1950.

State Historical Society of Colorado, "Ouray's Shirt Returns to Colorado," **Colorado Magazine,** Vol. 34, No. 3, July, 1957.

State Historical Society of Colorado, "Ute Indian Museum Dedication," **Colorado Magazine,** Vol. 33, No. 4, October, 1956.

Stewart, Omer C., "Ute Indians: Before and After White Contact," **Utah Historical Quarterly,** Vol. 34, No. 1, Winter, 1966.

Sumner, David, **Colorado/Southwest, the Land ... the People ... the History.** Denver, Colorado: Sanborn Souvenir Co., 1973.

Sumner, E.V., "Besieged By the Utes, The Massacre of 1879," Reprinted in Thomas C. Jones, Compiler, **Shaping the Spirit of America.** Chicago, Illinois: J.G. Ferguson, Co., 1964.

Townsend, R.B., **A Tenderfoot in Colorado.** Norman, Oklahoma: University of Oklahoma Press, New Edition, 1968.

Vandenbusche, Duane, **Early Days in the Gunnison Country.** Gunnison, Colorado: B & B Printers, 1974.

Vanderslice, Kurt and Ralph McBride, "Cantonment on the Uncompahgre," **Ptarmigan Quarterly.** Montrose, Colorado, Vol. 1, No. 3, 1976.

Urquhar, Lena M., **Colorow - The Angry Chieftain.** Denver, Colorado: Golden Bell Press, 1968.

Wellman, Paul I., **The Indian Wars of the West**. Garden City, New York: Doubleday & Co., 1947.

Whittier, Florence E., "The Grave of Chief Ouray," **Colorado Magazine**, Vol. 1, No. 7, November, 1924.

Wiegel, Mrs. C.W., "The Death of Ouray, Chief of the Utes," **Colorado Magazine**, Vol. 7, No. 5, September, 1930.

Wiegel, Mrs. C.W., "The Re-burial of Chief Ouray," **Colorado Magazine**, Vol. 5, No. 5, October, 1928.

Wood, Dorothy and Frances, **I Hauled These Mountains In Here**. Caldwell, Idaho: The Caxton Printers, Ltd., 1977.

Wormington, H.M. and Robert H. Lister, **Archaeological Investigations on the Uncompahgre Plateau**. Proceedings of Denver Museum of Natural History, No. 2, March, 1956.

INDEX

Abbott, Joseph B. 146
Abiquiu, New Mexico 34, 35, 38, 45, 49, 52, 56, 146, 147
Adams, Gov. Alva 197
Adams, C.E. 204
Adams, Charles 76, 88, 99, 103, 108, 109, 112-114, 122, 125, 131, 162-164, 171, 172, 174, 201
Ahanash 87
Alamosa, Colo. 68, 175
Alexander, Maj. A.J. 79, 104, 105
Anasazi 14
Animas River 94
Ankatosh 111
Antelope 71
Antonito, New Mexico 37
Apache Indians 14, 18, 34, 47, 52, 56, 57, 69, 99, 144
Arapaho Indians 18, 50, 56, 57, 61, 69, 109, 117
Arny, William 94, 99, 100
Arroyo Hondo 45
Augustine 195
Aztec Indians 14

Baker, Charles 93, 94
Baker's Park 93, 94, 99
Bates, Edgar G. 147
Battle of Milk Creek (See Meeker Massacre)
Bear Dance 16, 45-47, 76
Beaumont, S.B. 181
Beckwith, George 97, 144
Bell, Shannon Wilson 121
Bennett, Hiram P. 63, 74
Bent, Charles 38, 42
Bent, Ft. 38
Berry, William H. 177, 189
Bingham, Utah 118, 122, 123
Bishop, Nathan 107
Bitter Creek, Utah 195, 199, 201, 202
Black Canyon of the Gunnison 43, 45
Black Kettle 66, 69
Black Mare 45-47, 49, 52
Blanco 174
Blue Mesa 43
Bond, Henry F. 131, 133, 137
Boone, Col. Albert 74

Bowman 189
Brady, Joseph 161
Brady, Matthew 73, 100, 174
Breckenridge, Colo. 118, 123
Brunot, Felix 94, 99, 100, 107, 109, 110, 117
Brunot Treaty (See Treaty of 1873)
Buck, Antonio 182
Buckskin Charlie 174, 182, 184, 185, 200-204, 206, 207
Burns, Will 179

Cabazon, Jean "Frenchy" 125
Calhoun, James S. 38
Canon City, Colo. 130, 143
Cantonment on the Uncompahgre 190, 192
Capote 73
Capote Utes 19, 37, 39, 45, 52, 56, 73, 76, 99, 114, 146, 154, 181, 182
Captain Jack 71, 72, 74, 112, 143, 154, 158, 172, 174, 177
Carlisle Indian School 143
Carson, Kit 38, 42-44, 46, 49, 50, 54-56, 63, 68, 69, 72, 74, 75
Catz 115
Cebolla Valley 131
Chama, New Mexico 45
Chamberlain, William 142
Chavis 87
Cherry Creek 91
Cheta 205
Cheyenne Indians 18, 50, 61, 66, 69, 173
Cheyenne, Wyoming 109
Chilcott, George M. 74
Chipeta 13, 52, 55, 56, 58, 90, 103, 104, 112, 115, 120, 133, 134, 136, 137, 140, 141, 144, 147, 152, 156, 162, 165, 174, 175, 179, 184-186, 194-210
Chittendon, G.B. 135
Chivington, John M. 64, 66, 69, 173
Cimarron, New Mexico 56, 57, 144, 146, 147
Cimarron River 190
Cline, Capt. M.W. 162, 164, 187, 189
Clum, John P. 88
Cochetopa Creek 76
Cochetopa Pass 43, 79, 92, 124, 131

Craig, William 37
Crawford, Capt. Emmet 192
Cojoe 194
Colona, Colorado 131, 146
Colorado River 43, 45
Colorado Springs, Colo. 66, 78
Colorow 50, 71, 72, 76, 78, 97, 136, 143, 158, 162, 171, 174, 185, 190, 191, 193, 195, 197, 206
Comanche Indians 18, 59, 61, 68, 69
Conejos 52, 54, 56, 59, 61, 63, 65, 68, 83
Conejos River 49
Costilla 47
Cotoan (See Paron)
Cow Creek 190
Cradle Board 37
Crawford, Ft. 188, 192
Cree, Thomas 109, 114
Crockett, Ft. Davy 22, 37
Cummings, Gov. 68
Curecanti 113
Curtis, U.M. 72, 99, 112, 115

Dallas 148
Day, Dave 190
DeBeque, Colo. 163
Deer Creek 158
Del Norte, Colo. 105, 106, 193
Delta, Colo. 37, 123
Denver, Colo. 58, 59, 76, 77, 87, 92, 136
Denver Ute Agency 56, 76, 80, 81, 99, 136
Digger Indians 153
Doenhoff, Count 162
Dolan, Larry 122
Dolan, Thomas 109, 114
Dole, Stephen A. 122
Dolores River 94
Dominguez, Fray Atanasio 21
Doniphan, Col. 37, 38
Douglas 71, 72, 143, 154, 161-164, 166, 171, 174
Downer, James 122
Downing, Major 61
Dragon, Utah 199
Dresser, Frank 162
Duchesne, Ft. 199, 204
Duchesne River 190
Durango, Colo. 21, 146, 147, 151, 179
Dynamite 89

Elbert, Gov. 110
Engineer Mountain 99
Escalante, Fray Silvestre Velez de 21
Eskridge, Wilmer 158
Espanola, New Mexico 37
Evans, John 59, 61, 63, 64, 68

Fauntleroy, Col. T.T. 49
Fearheiler, Joe 94
Fetterman, Ft. 125
Fogg, Josiah 138

Fremont, John C. 39, 43, 45
French, Adnah 94, 96, 97
French, J. Carey 106
Friday, Chief 109
Friday, Ute (See Paron)
Fullerton, James 109

Garden of the Gods 27-31
Garfield, James A. 187
Garland, Ft. 69, 104, 190
Gerry, Melvin B. 128
Gilpin, Major William 38
Glenwood Springs, Colo. 195
Godfrey, William G. 73, 77
Grand Junction, Colo. 123, 176, 190, 191-193, 199
Grand Mesa 164, 166
Grand River 118, 165, 176, 191-193
Grand River Utes 20. 62. 73. 76. 195
Grant, Pres. U.S. 76, 91, 92, 103
Greeley, Colo. 154
Green River 37, 118, 123, 190
Greiner, John 43
Gross, F.A. 204
Guadalupe 49, 61
Guera Murah 34, 37, 152
Guero 111, 112, 134, 152
Gunnison, Colo. 65, 72, 84-86, 124, 127, 128, 131, 137, 188, 189
Gunnison, Capt. John W. 43, 45
Gunnison River 21, 43, 79, 121, 123, 165, 176, 189, 190, 191, 193

Hafen, LeRoy 68
Hartman, Alonzo 86, 121, 124, 134
Hartman, George 90
Hatch, Gen. Edward 102, 103, 147, 148, 165, 168, 170, 171, 172
Hayden, F.V. 135
Hayden Survey, 92, 95, 105, 131, 133, 135
Head, Lafayette 54, 56, 59, 61-63, 68, 73
Hersey, Rev. M.J. 204
Hill, N.P. 187
Holmes, W.H. 135
Holt, Charles F. 84
Hondo 115
Hopson, Dr. 179, 181, 182
Hot Stuff 89, 90, 143, 144
Howardsville, Colo. 93, 106
Hoyt, E.A. 158, 165
Huerfano Creek 69
Humphreys, James 121
Hunt, Alexander Gov. 72, 74
Hunt Treaty (See Treaty of 1868)
Hunter Act 198, 208
Hurlburt, George 147

Ignacio 72, 79, 106, 143, 146, 147, 149, 162, 174, 181, 207
Ignacio, Town of 179, 181, 184, 197-200, 202, 206
Indian Henry 188, 189

219

Ingersoll, Ernest 133, 135, 137
Irvine, Alexander G. 146

Jack of Clubs 89
Jackson, Andrew 187-189
Jackson, John H. 189
Jackson, William H. 40, 66, 92, 95, 98, 105, 107, 117, 119, 120, 131, 133-136, 142
James, Gen. Thomas 22, 24
Jicarilla Apache (See Apache)
Jocknick, Sidney 86-88, 112, 115, 121, 131, 134, 141
John 112
Johnson 71, 143, 154, 155, 157, 158, 162, 188
Johnson No. 2 112
Johnson, Tim 177
Julesburg, Colo. 61

Kaneache 49, 50, 53, 72, 79, 82, 100, 186
Kearny, Stephen W. 37, 38
Kellogg, Edward H. 73
Kelley, James P. 84, 121
Kendall, Jim 196, 197
Kerr, John 84
King, Mrs. W.G. 199
Kiowa (See Apache)
Kirkwood 187, 188

Lacey, Dr. John H. 143, 179, 181, 182
Lake City, Colo. 94, 99, 121, 123, 125-128, 144
Lang, John D. 92
La Plata Canyon 106
La Plata River 151, 192
Lauter, Herman 122
Lawrence, John 109
Leavenworth, Ft. 38, 175, 177
Lechat 23, 24
Left Hand 69
Lejanza, Gov. Martinez de 37
Lewis, Ft. 147, 151
Lincoln, Abraham 59, 66
Littlefield, J.S. 115
Littleton, Colo. 130
Los Animas River 97
Los Pinos Agency 76-107, 109, 113, 119-123, 125, 131, 133
Los Pinos II Agency (See Uncompahgre Agency)
Los Pinos River 73, 76, 147
Loutsenhizer, O.S. 121
Lupton, Ft. 56

Mac Kenzie, Gen. Ranold 99, 190-192
Mc Cook, Edward 77, 79, 81, 84, 85, 88, 89, 91, 92, 94, 97, 99, 100, 107, 140
Mc Cook, John 103, 179, 185, 200, 202-207
Mc Donald, Gen. John 92
Mc Farland, N.C. 147

Mc Kean, E.E. 203
Mc Kee 196

Mamie 201
Mancos River 94
Mannell 189
Manypenny, George 186, 187, 189
Mariano 140
Massachusetts, Ft. 48
Maxwell Ranch 56, 57
Meacham 87, 89
Mears, Otto 68, 83-85, 92, 103, 112, 113, 122, 125, 141, 144, 146, 174, 177, 186-190, 194
Meeker, Mrs. Arvilla Smith 156
Meeker, Josephine 154, 162, 164, 168
Meeker Massacre 148, 154-178, 185, 201
Meeker, Nathan C. 63, 154, 155, 157-160, 164, 166, 172, 173, 176
Meeker Uprising 10, 40, 74
Meriwether, David 46, 49, 50
Merritt, Wesley 161, 162
Mexican-American War 37
Mesa Verde 167
Milk Creek 158, 159, 161, 166, 172
Miller, Frank 121
Montrose, Colo. 43, 118, 123, 131, 141, 196, 198, 199, 203, 204, 207
Moreno 146
Mormons 38, 40
Morrill, Lot M. 147
Moss, Captain John 106
Mouache Utes 18, 45-50, 56, 57, 61, 62, 65, 73, 75, 76, 99, 114, 146, 154
Mountain Sheep 201

Naneese 185, 200, 202, 206
Navajo Indians 14, 17, 34, 52
Neva 109
Nevava 39, 50, 52, 55, 56, 71
Nicolay, John 63
Noon, George 121
Northern Utes 21, 40, 62, 71, 72, 112, 143

Oakes, D.C. 63, 72, 73, 83
Ojo Blanco 177
Ojo Caliente 37
Olathe, Colo. 190
Old Spanish Trail 34, 35
Ouray Agency 197
Owens, Hugh 204

Packer, Alferd 76, 118-130
Page, Henry 147, 179, 181
Pagosa Springs, Colo. 21, 147, 151, 154
Pahant 115
Paiute Indians 14, 17, 153
Palisade, Colo. 163
Parianuc Utes (See Grand River Utes)
Paron 52, 56, 57, 116, 117
Payne, Capt. 161

220

Pfeiffer, Col. Albert H.   87
Phillips, James   109
Piah   72, 76, 92, 98, 112, 134, 136
Pice, Flora   165
Pike's Peak   55
Pine River   179, 184, 206
Pinkerton Hot Springs   179
Pitkin, Gov. Frederick W.   148, 150, 157, 158, 165
Plateau Creek   163
Poncha Pass   85
Pope, Gen. John   192
Post, W.H.   164
Powder Face   116, 117
Price, Joseph   186, 200, 206
Price, Nathan   185, 186
Price, Col. Sterling   38
Pueblo, Ft.   47

Queashegut   52
Quenche   35, 37, 64
Quiziachigiate   39

Randolph, J.A.   125, 126
Rangely, Colo.   195
Rankin, Joe   161
Raton Pass   38, 49
Rawlins, Wyo.   109, 159
Reagan, Albert   203
Red Canyon   160
Red River   45
Reese, D.   106
Rico, Colo.   94
Ridgway, Colo.   102, 138
Rio Arriba   37
Rio Grande   110
Rivera, Juan Maria de   21
Robideaux, Antoine   22, 37, 45
Rockwell, Wilson   143
Rosas, Gov. Luis de   17
Ruffner, E.H.   95, 106
Rusling, Gen.   68
Russell, S.A.   84, 146, 189

Saguache, Colo.   49, 76, 77, 83-85, 113, 121-125, 146, 189
Saguache Pass   (See Cochetopa Pass)
St. Joseph, Missouri   59
Saint Vrain, Col. Ceran   49
Salt Lake City, Utah   118
Salvador   (See Guera Murah)
San Juan Mountains   55, 89, 93, 94, 97, 99, 102, 105, 110, 114, 115, 117, 144, 148, 165
San Luis Valley   47, 65, 66, 72, 85
Sand Creek Massacre   66, 69, 158, 172
Santa Fe, New Mexico   17, 34, 38, 99
Sapinero, Colo.   131
Sapovanero   87, 90, 100, 103, 162, 164, 178, 195
Saunders, William   140, 162, 172

Sawaich   74
Sawawatsewich   87
Scalp Dance   76, 136
Schiel, Jacob H.   45
Schurz, Carl   153, 162, 172-175, 186, 187
Sells, Cato   201
Seven Nations   18
Severo   174
Shafer, Sheldon   94
Shavano   49, 50, 53, 71, 79, 87, 110, 111, 162, 174, 187-189
Shavano, Johnson   189
Sherman, George   162
Sherman, Gen. W.T.   88, 89
Shining Mountains   26
Shoshone Indians   14, 17
Silverton, Colo.   93, 94
Sioux Indians   18, 50, 56, 57, 109
Smith, Dr. E.F.   179
Snake Indians   14
South Platte River   61
Southern Ute Indians   19, 40, 49, 50, 63, 72, 79, 106, 112, 143, 146, 147, 167, 168, 174, 176, 178, 179, 181, 186, 192, 197-199, 204, 208
Sowerwich   72, 158, 174
Speer, Lt. Calvin T.   82, 84, 86, 88
Stanley, Agent H.   165, 168
Steck, Michael   45, 63
Steele, Ft. Wyoming   158, 159, 166
Stony Pass   105
Suckett   89
Susan   37, 40, 56, 103, 112, 157, 162, 164
Suvata   185, 204
Swan, Israel   121
Swartze, John   125

Tabeguache Ute Indians   19, 34, 43, 45, 49, 52, 55, 56, 61-66, 72, 73, 75, 76, 80, 82, 87, 88, 99, 143, 167, 168, 174, 176, 178, 186, 189, 192, 194
Tabnchakot   115
Taos, New Mexico   17, 34, 35, 37-39, 42, 43, 49, 55-57
Tappan, Col.   64
Tapuch   177
Taylor Park   85, 134, 137
Teller, Henry M.   153, 187
Tepee (erection of)   27-31
Thomas, Gov. Charles   129, 130
Thompson, James B.   35, 76, 81, 94, 99, 108, 112, 115
Thompson, Phillip   37
Thornburgh, Maj. Thomas T.   112, 158-161, 166, 172, 174
Tierra Amarilla, New Mexico   56
Tierra Blanco   47, 49
Tomichi Creek   43
Toomuchagut   194
Towaoc   181
Townsend, R.B.   77-79

Trask, Jabez Nelson 86-88, 96, 108
Treaty of 1849 38, 39
Treaty of 1855 49
Treaty of 1862 59
Treaty of 1863 59, 61-66, 73
Treaty of 1868 63, 66, 72-77, 103
Treaty of 1873 57, 58, 66, 91-117, 146
Treaty of 1880 176-179, 186-190
Tusaquinot (See Piah)

Uinta River 22, 56
Uintah Reservation 176, 190
Uintah Ute Indians 21, 56, 62, 77, 167, 197
Unaneanance 84
Uncompahgre Agency 131-153, 168, 177, 179, 182
Uncompahgre, Ft. 22, 37
Uncompahgre Park 102, 115, 131, 137, 148
Uncompahgre Peak 26
Uncompahgre Plateau 21, 43
Uncompahgre River 21, 43, 134, 146, 164, 190, 191, 198
Uncompahgre Ute Indians (See Tabeguache Indians)
Ute Friday 57
Ute Indian Museum 15, 22, 141, 205
Ute Mountain 199
Ute Mountain Ute Indians 167, 181, 199, 208
Ute Pass 56

Ute-Ulay Mine 94

Vack Creek 199
Valois 172
Vickers, William B. 150, 153, 157

Wanztiz 115
Wara 73
Warency 111
Washington 112
Washington, D.C. 59, 63, 72, 73, 83, 87, 103, 111, 112, 137, 144, 170-172, 174-177, 181, 201
Watts, Babe 203, 206
Wattseonavot 161
Wayt, L.M. 202, 204, 206
Weeminuche Ute Indians 19, 56, 73, 76, 99, 114, 146, 149, 154, 181
Wheeler, W.D. 137, 148
White Antelope 69
White River 76, 154, 190
White River Agency 155, 158, 162, 166, 168
White River Ute Indians 40, 63, 76, 99, 143, 154, 162, 167, 171, 174, 176, 178, 181
Whitely, Simeon 62
Woretsiz 174

Yagnah 204
Yampa River 21, 72, 190
Yampa Ute Indians 21, 73, 76